W9-CPN-316

D0859411

BEN ROETHLISBERGER

SPORTS STARS
who give back

GIFTED AND GIVING FOOTBALL STAR

by Tom Robinson

Enslow Publishers, Inc.
40 Industrial Road
Box 398
Berkeley Heights, NJ 07922
USA
http://www.enslow.com

Library of Congress Cataloging-in-Publication Data
Robinson, Tom.
  Ben Roethlisberger : gifted and giving football star / Tom Robinson.
     p. cm. — (Sports stars who give back)
  Includes bibliographical references and index.
  Summary: "A biography of American football player Ben Roethlisberger, focusing on his philanthropic activities off the field"–Provided by publisher.
  ISBN 978-0-7660-3590-4
  1. Roethlisberger, Ben, 1982—Juvenile literature. 2. Football players—United States—Biography—Juvenile literature. 3. Philanthropists—United States—Biography—Juvenile literature. I. Title.
  GV939.R623R63 2010
  796.332092—dc22
  [B]
                                        2009026187

Printed in the United States of America

102009 Lake Book Manufacturing, Inc., Melrose Park, IL

10 9 8 7 6 5 4 3 2 1

To Our Readers: We have done our best to make sure all Internet addresses in this book were active and appropriate when we went to press. However, the author and the publisher have no control over and assume no liability for the material available on those Internet sites or on other Web sites they may link to. Any comments or suggestions can be sent by e-mail to comments@enslow.com or to the address on the back cover.

♻ Enslow Publishers, Inc. is committed to printing our books on recycled paper. The paper in every book contains between 10% to 30% post-consumer waste (PCW). The cover board on the outside of each book contains 100% PCW. Our goal is to do our part to help young people and the environment too!

Photo credits: Keith Srakocic/AP Images, 1, 46, 67; Michael Conroy/AP Images, 8; David J. Phillip/AP Images, 12; J.D. Pooley/AP Images, 18; Howard Moyer/AP Images, 20; Jeffrey A. Camarati/AP Images, 25; Peter Cosgrove/AP Images, 28; Dave Martin/AP Images, 33; LM Otero/AP Images, 38; Ed Betz/AP Images, 43; Chris Gardner/AP Images, 48; Al Behrman/AP Images, 60; Denis Poroy/AP Images, 63; Philip G. Pavely/AP Images, 70; John Amis/AP Images, 75; Gene J. Puskar/AP Images, 82, 106; Francis Specker/AP Images, 84; Ken Blaze/AP Images, 88; Tom Gannam/AP Images, 92; Paul Sakuma/AP Images, 98; Chris O'Meara/AP Images, 111

Cover Photo: Keith Srakocic/AP Images

CONTENTS

SUPER BOWL CHAMP

Offensive practice for the Pittsburgh Steelers hit a boring stretch at times. The team practiced its trick plays all throughout the 2005 season, but they never seemed to use them. As it turns out, the Steelers were waiting for the perfect time.

That time came on February 5, 2006, in Super Bowl XL. The Steelers were leading the Seattle Seahawks 14–10 midway through the fourth quarter. But Pittsburgh still needed that extra something to pull away. With first down on Seattle's 43-yard line, the Steelers finally ran a trick play.

It started innocently enough. Second-year quarterback Ben Roethlisberger handed the ball off to running back Willie Parker. Then, Parker handed the ball to wide receiver Antwaan Randle El in what looked like a reverse. But Randle El stopped running and looked to pass. He spotted wide receiver Hines Ward downfield and fired a pass in his direction. Ward caught the ball and ran it into the end zone. That 43-yard touchdown clinched the Steelers' 21–10 victory.

The unique players on Pittsburgh's offense were vital in making that play succeed. Randle El was a quarterback at Indiana University, which helped him throw a good pass to Ward. Roethlisberger was six-foot-five and 241 pounds, bigger than the typical quarterback. His size helped him throw a strong block that gave Randle El enough time to throw. The combination of Randle El's arm and Roethlisberger's strength helped make it a perfect play at a perfect time. "The guys get tired of practicing those plays because we never call them," Steelers offensive coordinator Ken Whisenhunt said. "They were in the right defense, and it felt like the right time."[1]

RELATIVE YOUNGSTER

The quarterback position usually requires the poise and experience of a veteran. In 2006, Roethlisberger, at age twenty-three, became the youngest starting quarterback to ever win a Super Bowl.

Roethlisberger threw the ball well in the playoffs, but his passing statistics in the Super Bowl were disappointing. He completed just 9 of 21 attempts

YOUNGEST SUPER BOWL STARTING QUARTERBACKS

Roethlisberger was the second youngest quarterback in NFL history to start a Super Bowl. Only Dan Marino was younger. Marino, who grew up in Pittsburgh before a Hall of Fame career with the Miami Dolphins, lost the Super Bowl in his second season and never made it back. Roethlisberger said that Marino, who was also twenty-three for his Super Bowl appearance but seven months younger, told him: "On one hand, enjoy it. Have a good time. But take it seriously enough that you want to win it because you never know when it's going to happen again."

for 123 yards with no touchdowns and 2 interceptions. The quarterback had to find other ways to help his team to victory, such as running. Roethlisberger was able to run up field and gain yards for the Steelers' offense. He was also effective at scrambling, or running away from defenders while looking at his passing options.

TAKING THE LEAD

The Steelers were fortunate to escape the first quarter trailing only 3–0. Roethlisberger passed for a single yard while going 1-for-5. But the Steelers finally took the lead in the second quarter, when Roethlisberger was effective in both kinds of running.

Starting at their own 41-yard line, Roethlisberger began driving the Steelers down the field. It was promising when Roethlisberger completed a pass for 20 yards. But after an incomplete pass, the Steelers were called for a penalty and Roethlisberger was sacked. Pittsburgh faced third-and-28 from the Seahawks' 40.

On the next play, Seattle's pass rush forced Roethlisberger to scramble. If he was able to gain a few yards with his feet, the Steelers might have reached field goal range and been able to tie the game. The quarterback wanted more. Just as Roethlisberger approached the line of scrimmage, he slowed and moved sideways. Since he remained in the backfield, Roethlisberger could still throw a forward pass. From there, Roethlisberger threw the ball across the field to Ward. Ward jumped up and fought for the ball, coming down with a 37-yard catch at the Seahawks' 3-yard line. Then Steelers running back Jerome Bettis ran the ball twice, powering his way to the 1. After the two-minute warning, it was third-and-goal on the 1.

Roethlisberger faked a pitch to Bettis on third down. He then cut back toward the middle and jumped, reaching for the goal line. Seattle linebacker D. D. Lewis was there, but not in time. Roethlisberger reached the end zone, securing the touchdown and the Steelers' 7–3 lead with 1:55 left in the half.

Roethlisberger scrambles away from Seattle's Bryce Fisher in Super Bowl XL.

HOLDING ON

On the second play of the second half, Parker hit a hole and did not stop, going for 75 yards and a touchdown. It was the longest touchdown run in Super Bowl history. The Steelers' lead grew to 14–3. The Seahawks would come back midway through the third quarter, however. Roethlisberger threw an interception, and a few plays later Seattle quarterback Matt Hasselbeck threw a 16-yard touchdown pass to Jerramy Stevens to make the score 14–10. But that was as close as the Seahawks would get.

After the trick play in the fourth quarter gave the Steelers a 21–10 lead, they needed to stop the Seahawks and run the remaining time off the clock.

DRIVING THE BUS

Roethlisberger got some of the credit for convincing Jerome "The Bus" Bettis to return for one more season in 2005. Bettis, the fifth-leading rusher in NFL history, was happy he held off on retirement. He was with the Steelers for their 21–10 Super Bowl XL victory over the Seattle Seahawks in his hometown of Detroit, Michigan. The only Super Bowl Bettis ever won in his thirteen-year career came in his final game. "It was absolutely awesome to come up here and win one for Jerome," Roethlisberger said.

The defense did the job. Roethlisberger helped with the latter. With four minutes left, he ran for a first down on third-and-three in Steelers territory. Now it would be even harder for Seattle to score two touchdowns.

Roethlisberger finished the game with seven carries for 25 yards. He was hardly worried that his passing statistics were below his usual standard. He had won the Super Bowl as a twenty-three-year-old.

"We got the win and that's all that matters," he said.[2]

PITTSBURGH CELEBRATES

The win over the Seahawks restored one of the National Football League's most famous franchises to its previous level of glory. Pittsburgh won four Super Bowls between the 1974 and 1979 seasons, winning back-to-back titles twice. The fifth Super Bowl ring—dubbed as "one for the thumb"—matched the most by any team.

The team had come close since the 1979 season. In coach Bill Cowher's fourteen seasons in Pittsburgh, the Steelers reached the American Football Conference championship game six times. The winner of that game goes to the Super Bowl. One of the appearances was the previous season, when Roethlisberger was a rookie.

> "We got the win and that's all that matters."
>
> —Ben Roethlisberger

BEST SUPER BOWL RECORDS (AS OF 2009)

Team	W–L
Pittsburgh Steelers	6–1
San Francisco 49ers	5–0
Dallas Cowboys	5–3
Green Bay Packers	3–1
New England Patriots	3–2
Oakland/Los Angeles Raiders	3–2
Washington Redskins	3–2

They reached the Super Bowl in 1996, but lost 27–17 to the Dallas Cowboys.

The Steelers came into the 2006 AFC Championship game as an underdog. Pittsburgh had stormed back from a 7–5 record to reach the playoffs by winning its last four regular-season games. The Steelers were the sixth seed of six teams in the AFC playoffs, but they went on the road and won three straight playoff games. Even though Seattle was the top-seeded team in the National Football Conference playoffs and had the highest-scoring offense in

Super Bowl XL was not Roethlisberger's best day throwing the ball.

the league, the Steelers were actually considered the favorite in the Super Bowl.

None of that changed Roethlisberger's approach. He thrived on pulling off the late-season surprises. "We still see ourselves as underdogs," he said. "We always have."[3]

With a quarterback some said was too young finding ways to contribute to unlikely plays, the underdog Steelers won their fifth Super Bowl. Roethlisberger's career was just getting started, and there would be more success to come.

MAKING IT COUNT

After three years, Ben Roethlisberger had never started a high school football game as quarterback. But Terry Hoeppner, the head coach at Miami University in Ohio, was still thinking about offering him a scholarship. Before Ben's senior season, Hoeppner invited him to the Miami summer camp to watch him play quarterback. Hoeppner was impressed by what he saw.

One game into Ben's senior season, Hoeppner was convinced. Ben fired 6 touchdown passes against Elida High in his first varsity start at quarterback. Hoeppner offered a scholarship the next day. "We waited until he played a game," Hoeppner said. "I didn't want to be the genius to offer this guy who never played quarterback a scholarship."[1] Ben made the final decision easy with his big first game. "I said, 'That's good enough for me,'" said Hoeppner, who died in 2007.[2]

Hoeppner was not the first to see potential in the young football, baseball, and basketball player as he grew up in Findlay, Ohio. The town's mayor, Tony Iriti, coached Ben in football when he was in fifth and sixth grade and was a volunteer assistant coach during Ben's time at Findlay High School. "You usually don't expect a kid to make every play, but Ben always seemed to make things work. He has a lot of God-given talent and natural ability."[3]

FATHER'S INFLUENCE

Ben was born March 2, 1982, in Lima, Ohio. His parents, Ken and Ida Roethlisberger, divorced when he was eighteen months old. As a young boy, Ben lived with his father and saw his mother every other

FINDLAY, OHIO

Roethlisberger's hometown is in the northwestern part of Ohio, about forty-five miles (seventy-two km) south of Toledo. Findlay had an estimated population of 39,118, as of 2005. Findlay High School, which has an average graduating class of 500 students, has produced Ohio High School Athletic Association state champions in baseball (1971), boys' basketball (1948), boys' cross country (1974), boys' golf (1984), boys' ice hockey (1978, 1983), and boys' swimming and diving (1944).

weekend. Ken remarried when Ben was four years old and Ben calls Ken's second wife, Brenda, "Mom."

When Ben was eight years old, he started shooting baskets at his hoop in the driveway while waiting for his mother to pick him up. Hours passed, but Ida never made it. She had been in a serious automobile accident. After being on life support for weeks, she passed away from the injuries suffered in the accident. "That time had a profound effect on Ben," said Brenda Roethlisberger, a yoga instructor and substitute teacher. "His dad was so composed and collected, he became Ben's hero. That's whom he began to pattern himself after."[4]

Ken played quarterback in college before a knee injury slowed him down. He ended up switching to baseball, and he played shortstop at Georgia Tech. Ben credits his father's calm demeanor for

> **"His dad was so composed and collected, he became Ben's hero.**
>
> —*Brenda Roethlisberger*

PAYING TRIBUTE

Roethlisberger points to the sky after every touchdown. He is pointing toward heaven, in acknowledgment of his mother, Ida.

Nike hung a poster of Roethlisberger's high school picture in Findlay in 2006.

helping Ben thrive as a quarterback. "I've always had a sense of calmness," he said. "I've been surrounded by it my whole life. It's a tribute to my dad, the most cool, calm, and collected person I know."[5]

PATIENT APPROACH

Ben showed patience. Although he was an outstanding athlete and an all-star and captain in all three sports, he had to wait until his senior year at Findlay

Carlee Roethlisberger, Ben's younger sister, continued the family's athletic tradition. Carlee joined her father and brother as National Collegiate Athletic Association (NCAA) Division I athletes, and her mother, Brenda, as women's college basketball players. Carlee, a six-foot, one-inch sophomore, was the second player off the bench at the University of Oklahoma in 2008–09. She averaged 6 points per game for the Sooners, who were ranked in the top ten in the nation.

At Findlay High School, Carlee led the team to the state semifinals as a senior, and she was named Ohio Division I Player of the Year. Carlee, the school's all-time leading scorer in basketball with more than 1,600 points, could have also played volleyball in college. She helped Findlay go unbeaten in the Greater Buckeye Conference for all four years and was recruited by top programs like Nebraska and Minnesota, among others.

Carlee was a first-team all-state selection in two sports in high school. "I think it's always important to make my own way and do it myself," Carlee said. "I have goals that I want to reach and I don't want them to be just because of my brother. I'm proud of all the things he's done. I love being Ben's sister. He has a positive image. But if I can work my own way up and make my own name that would be great."

High School to reach the top of the quarterback depth chart.

Ben loved all three sports, and he was good at them, too. In baseball, he played shortstop and hit .300 in high school. He did so well on the basketball court—averaging 26.5 points, 9 rebounds, and 5 assists per game as a high school senior—that Ben

Roethlisberger shakes hands with his former coach, Cliff Hite, at a Findlay game in 2005.

once believed basketball would be his sport in college.

In football, the future Super Bowl–winning quarterback waited in the wings as a wide receiver and backup quarterback before his senior season. He never complained when Ryan Hite, the son of head coach Cliff Hite, held on to the starting quarterback position. The skilled three-sport athlete played quarterback on the junior varsity team as a freshman and sophomore, and then moved to wide receiver on the varsity team while he waited for his chance to run the team.

Hite is sometimes compared with Pop Harrington. The E.A. Laney High School basketball coach in Wilmington, North Carolina, cut Michael Jordan from the varsity team as a sophomore. "I might be as infamous as Michael Jordan's coach," Hite said. "You know, Ryan did break the school passing record. Of course, Ben doubled it the next year."[6] Ryan Hite went on to be an all-conference player at Division III Denison University, but only after switching to wide receiver.

TAKING ADVANTAGE

Once inserted as the starting quarterback, Ben made the most of his chance. He did not stop with his 6-touchdown game to open the season. Soon, the famed football program at Ohio State joined Miami of Ohio in the recruiting race. Ben threw for 4,041 yards and 54 touchdowns, ran for 7 touchdowns, and took Findlay into the state playoffs. The Trojans finished 10–2. When it was time to vote for Mr. Football, the top high school football player in Ohio, for 1999, Ben finished second. The *Associated Press* gave the award to St. Peter Chanel's Brandon Childress. Childress went on to help Ohio State win a national championship before playing cornerback in the NFL for the New England Patriots and Philadelphia Eagles.

Ben was named Ohio's Division I Offensive Player of the Year in his high school senior season. That gave him the chance to play in two prestigious all-star games the next summer. In addition to playing in Ohio's North-South Game, where he threw 2 touchdown passes, Ben also quarterbacked the Ohio team against Pennsylvania in the annual Big 33 Football Classic. At the 2000 game in Hershey, Pennsylvania, Pennsylvania beat Ohio, 31–14. But Roethlisberger later helped the Big 33 continue its legacy of having at least one alumni of the Big 33 game in every Super Bowl.

Guyton Giannotta was Ben's host family "father" for the week of practice leading up to the all-star game in Hershey. He remembers a skinny but driven player. Roethlisberger weighed just 175 pounds at the time, but he knew what he wanted from his football career. Giannotta hosts players each year and always asks them what they want to do with their life. "Ben is the only one who looked at me and said, 'Mr. G, my goal in life is to play on Sunday afternoon,'" Giannotta said.

Ohio State thought Ben might be a receiver, possibly as a tight end, in college. When he looked at Miami, Ben saw an opportunity to be the starting quarterback after one season, when Mike Bath graduated. "It came down to what would be comfortable for me and what felt right," Roethlisberger said. "I prayed a lot about it, talked to my family about it, and it seemed like the right fit."[7]

COLLEGE CAREER

Ben Roethlisberger passed up the chance to play at Ohio State, a program that is almost always nationally ranked and playing in bowl games. Instead he chose Miami University of Ohio, and he helped the RedHawks achieve many of those same honors. Before he could start though, Roethlisberger again had to wait his turn.

Roethlisberger likely knew that he would have to wait when he committed. Miami had fifth-year senior Mike Bath returning to start at quarterback. This would give Roethlisberger time to adjust to college football. If he took a redshirt and did not play as a true freshman, Roethlisberger could also save that year of eligibility to use later.

TOUGH DECISION

Roethlisberger was practicing with Miami and in uniform for each game during his true freshman season. The plan was, if he was not needed, Roethlisberger would redshirt and save all four years of his college eligibility. Miami and Roethlisberger nearly had to change plans during a game against Ohio State. "I had a fifth-year quarterback in Mike Bath and I also didn't want to play anybody before they were ready," Miami coach Terry Hoeppner said. "But, ironically, in our game against Ohio State, Mike got knocked down and Mike's on the ground and the trainer's with him and I turn to Ben, 'Buckle up. Get ready.' And he starts throwing on the sideline. And, if he goes in, he's not coming out. It was close, really close, but he didn't have to get in there."[1] When Roethlisberger was not needed against the Buckeyes, Hoeppner was able to stick with his intention of saving his top recruit for the following season.

COLLEGE DEBUT

After sitting out the entire 2000 season as a redshirt, Roethlisberger won the starting quarterback position prior to the 2001 season. He took control of the team from opening day and led Miami, a member of the Mid-American Conference (MAC), against two opponents from the more prestigious Big Ten Conference. Roethlisberger and the RedHawks struggled on the road against Michigan and Iowa.

Roethlisberger celebrates a third-quarter touchdown against North Carolina in 2002.

"It might have helped to be thrown into the fire that early versus Michigan and Iowa, because really, the light turned on," Miami offensive coordinator and quarterbacks coach Shane Montgomery said.[2] Roethlisberger showed that in his first college home

TRIPLE THREAT

In addition to passing and running, Roethlisberger made contributions at Miami University as a punter. He specialized in placing the ball in the "coffin corner," inside the 20-yard line. Roethlisberger was often called on to punt when the team was near midfield during his second and third seasons. He placed 17 of his 24 career college punts inside the opponent's 20. His best season was as a sophomore in 2002, when Roethlisberger averaged 43.8 yards and put 9 of 12 punts inside the 20.

game when he connected on 20 of 25 passes for 264 yards and 2 touchdowns. He ran for the RedHawks' other score in a 21–14 win over Cincinnati.

Establishing himself as an accurate drop-back passer with a strong arm, Roethlisberger also showed the ability to throw on the move. Miami's offense was built to suit his abilities and was similar to what Roethlisberger ran in high school. The RedHawks often used a moving pocket. This allowed Roethlisberger to slide in either direction and avoid pressure while throwing short passes.

Roethlisberger credited his experience playing other sports and other positions with helping him reach his potential. Playing shortstop in baseball helped him throw on the run. Being a basketball point guard helped him make quick decisions when plays did not go exactly as planned. Reading defensive coverages in football was easier after having been a wide receiver. Still, there was nothing like playing quarterback. "I love being quarterback," he said. "I want to be in the position where I can have the ball in my hands every play. I like having the ball in my hands at the end of the game. I like directing things and being a leader and leading by example."[3]

Before long, Roethlisberger was setting records and engineering comeback victories. He threw for a school record 399 yards, including a game-winning, 70-yard "Hail Mary" touchdown pass as time expired to beat Akron 30–28. Miami wiped out a 21–7 halftime deficit against Ohio when Roethlisberger completed 24-of-37 passes for 322 yards and 5 touchdowns in a 36–24 win. He picked apart the Hawaii blitz package while setting school single-game records in each passing category with 40 completions in 53 attempts for 452 yards during a 52–51 loss.

Roethlisberger finished the season as the most productive freshman quarterback in the country and

THE NICKNAME

Roethlisberger picked up the nickname "Big Ben" after succeeding on one of the most famous plays of his college career. When a team is desperate late in a game it will sometimes call a "Hail Mary." This is when the quarterback throws the ball as high and as far as he can and hopes somebody catches it. In Miami's playbook, the play was called "Big Ben." Miami connected on the play October 13, 2001, with Roethlisberger throwing to Eddie Tillitz on the game's final play for a 30–28 victory over Akron.

Roethlisberger finds space as he looks for a receiver against Central Florida in 2003.

as the second-leading passer in the MAC with 3,105 yards and 25 touchdowns. He set just about every Miami season passing record while earning honors as a second-team conference all-star, the

MAC Freshman of the Year, and as a first-team Football Writers' Association of America Freshman All-American.

FEELING COMFORTABLE

Roethlisberger could see progress coming during his redshirt sophomore season when he set more school records and threw for 3,238 yards and 22 touchdowns. He said he "started to feel comfortable with the way things were going in the offensive system and everything that was unfolding at Miami."[4]

The RedHawks put up a fight in a 29–24 loss to third-ranked Iowa when Roethlisberger passed for 343 yards and 3 touchdowns. Later in the season, Roethlisberger threw for conference records of 41 completions and 525 yards, along with 4 touchdowns in a 48–41 loss to Northern Illinois.

Miami won six out of seven in the middle of the season, but lost its final two games to finish 7–5. Included in the late losses was a 36–34 defeat at Marshall, the third loss of the season against a ranked team.

THE BIG FINISH

Roethlisberger opened his junior season as a longshot candidate for the Heisman Trophy, which is awarded to college football's most outstanding player. The award is difficult to win for a player in a small-school conference, so just getting into the debate was an accomplishment. The season did not start as planned, though. Roethlisberger threw 4 interceptions during a 21–3 loss to Iowa. But that wound up being the last time Roethlisberger and Miami were disappointed in the 2003 season.

Miami scored at least 33 points in every game the rest of the season, hitting the 40-point mark in all but two. Roethlisberger spent the season breaking his own school records. He also led the RedHawks into the national rankings with thirteen straight wins, a MAC championship, and a victory over Louisville in the GMAC Bowl.

FINAL COLLEGE GAME

Speculation ran rampant in the days leading up to the GMAC Bowl about whether Roethlisberger would end his college career one year early and declare himself eligible for the NFL draft. Pundits discussed where Roethlisberger would stand in comparison to Eli Manning and other quarterbacks if he decided

ABOUT MIAMI UNIVERSITY OF OHIO

Miami is a public university that was founded in 1809 and named after the Miami Indian tribe that inhabited the area. The campus is based in Oxford, thirty-five miles (fifty-six km) north of Cincinnati. As of the fall of 2008, Miami had 14,488 undergraduate students and 1,812 graduate students on the Oxford campus. Miami's sports teams, nicknamed the RedHawks, compete in the Mid-American Conference.

to forgo his senior season. Roethlisberger and his family met with Hoeppner in the days leading up to the game to discuss the possibilities. They told the rest of the Miami team the night before that the bowl game would be Roethlisberger's last as a college player.

The decision about his future did not disrupt Roethlisberger's preparation for Miami's first bowl game in seventeen years. Roethlisberger then went out and made his final college game a special one. The RedHawks took the field against Louisville with the nation's longest winning streak at twelve games. By halftime, Roethlisberger had already thrown for 4 touchdowns while helping Miami build a 35–7 second-quarter lead. He finished with 376 yards passing to lead the fourteenth-ranked RedHawks to a 49–28 victory over Louisville.

HISTORIC COMBINATION

Roethlisberger joined NFL players Byron Leftwich and Chad Pennington as the only Mid-American Conference quarterbacks to reach 11,000 career yards in total offense. He also set conference records for completions (342), passing yards (4,486), and total offense (4,597) in a season during his final year in 2003.

> ❝He made some plays that made those of you who haven't seen him play in person go, 'How can he do that?'❞
>
> —Terry Hoeppner

Roethlisberger twice slipped away from what looked like sacks and fired tough passes right on target. "He made some plays that made those of you who haven't seen him play in person go, 'How can he do that? How can he keep escaping like that and hitting guys in the hands with balls?'" Hoeppner said.[5]

Roethlisberger was 16-for-20 for 291 yards in a special first half. When Louisville (9–4) started to get close, he led the RedHawks to two more touchdowns in the fourth quarter.

After the game, he announced his decision to leave school for the NFL. When Roethlisberger left, the program was tied for its longest winning streak (thirteen games), matching a run put together in the 1972 to 1974 seasons. In his final five college games, he threw 19 touchdown passes and just 1 interception.

Roethlisberger threw 4 touchdowns as Miami-Ohio beat Louisville in the GMAC Bowl.

4

DRAFT SEASON

When Ben Roethlisberger was preparing for his junior season at Miami University of Ohio, he unknowingly saw into his future. He visited the Cincinnati Bengals training camp to watch another big, strong-armed quarterback—top draft pick Carson Palmer. "I wanted to see Carson play," Roethlisberger said. "I wanted to just kind of see how his demeanor is and how he plays. He's really impressive. That's the ultimate goal, to get out here and play on Sundays."[1]

Roethlisberger took another step toward playing on Sundays when he decided to forgo his fourth college football season and become eligible for the NFL Draft. When he made his decision that

December, Roethlisberger had heard enough experts weigh in to be reasonably sure that he would be picked in the top half of the first round. Projections placed Roethlisberger anywhere from the very top of an impressive group of quarterbacks to somewhere in the top ten to fifteen overall selections in the draft.

Before he could find out which team selected him and where he would start his professional career, Roethlisberger had to go through the pre-draft processes of meeting with teams and being tested in various workouts.

EARLY PREPARATIONS

When Roethlisberger made his announcement that he would become a professional, many potential agents began making offers. Some were more credible than others. Roethlisberger agreed to be

DID YOU KNOW?

Roethlisberger acknowledged one of his dreams as a youngster was to have his jersey retired from his high school, college, and professional teams. He is already two-thirds of the way to that goal after Findlay High School and Miami University of Ohio retired his No. 7 jerseys. Once a jersey is retired, no other players are allowed to wear it for that team in the future.

SPECIAL HELP

When Roethlisberger traveled to California for some additional training before the NFL Draft, his agent arranged for one of his favorite players from his boyhood days to help out—former NFL quarterback Warren Moon. "He needed to work on getting away from center because he worked out of the shotgun in college so much," Moon said.

represented by Leigh Steinberg and Steinberg's associate, Ryan Tollner. Days later, on January 5, 2004, Roethlisberger made the temporary move to Newport Beach, California, to begin training so he was as prepared as possible for his draft workouts.

Steinberg set up Roethlisberger in a luxury condo and arranged for two months of private training. The training included weightlifting and other workouts at a gym. It also included sessions with quarterback coach Steve Clarkson. He worked on improving Roethlisberger's throwing technique and footwork. Roethlisberger came away from the training feeling much stronger, saying the difference in his body was "like night and day."[2]

WATCHED CLOSELY

As the draft gets closer, NFL teams like to get a close look at potential picks. The teams measure and time the players, put them through drills and get to know them through interviews and written tests. Depending on the circumstances and how high they might be picked, this is done with large groups of players at events called "combines." The workouts are arranged for that player to be seen by many teams or in private workouts.

Roethlisberger attended the NFL Combine in Indianapolis, Indiana, in February, but that did not necessarily improve his status. He was unable to stand out from the pack of other quarterbacks there. The San Diego Chargers held the first pick and were considering taking a quarterback. Roethlisberger was rated near the top with Mississippi's Eli Manning and North Carolina State's Philip Rivers. So the Chargers arranged to come to Ohio to watch Roethlisberger in a private workout.

NFL DRAFT HISTORY

Bert Bell, who later became NFL commissioner, came up with the plan for the draft that owners approved May 19, 1935. The draft called for the weaker teams to get the first choice of top college prospects, with teams picking in reverse order up until the defending champion picked last. Jay Berwanger, the first Heisman Trophy winner, was the first player ever selected in an NFL draft.

The first draft was held in Philadelphia at the Ritz-Carlton Hotel on February 8, 1936. The Philadelphia Eagles chose Berwanger, a halfback from the University of Chicago. Philadelphia wound up trading the rights to Berwanger to the Chicago Bears, but Berwanger never played pro football.

Eli Manning of Mississippi was another top-rated college quarterback.

Chargers owner Alex Spanos, general manager A. J. Smith, coach Marty Schottenheimer and offensive coordinator Cam Cameron observed as Roethlisberger tried to show the team he could be the right choice for the elite status as No. 1 pick.

Miami University coach Terry Hoeppner arranged the workout to showcase his players to the professional scouts. Roethlisberger was the showcase. Hoeppner said any doubts that could have been created by Roethlisberger's performance at the combine in Indianapolis were wiped out by his effort at home. "The people who know the game, I don't think it affected them," Hoeppner said of the combine. "All today did was either confirm or convince people that he's a special player. He's fast, he's accurate, he's strong. He has incredible touch. He can throw the ball the length of the football field. Other than that, I don't know what you want in a quarterback."[3]

NO CHOICE

Top first-round draft picks have the potential of winding up on bad teams because the worst teams usually get to pick first (unless they trade their pick). Many highly regarded quarterbacks entered the NFL on poor teams that were unable to support and protect them right away.

During the time leading up to the draft, Roethlisberger repeatedly stated that he was not concerned with which team selected him. Eli Manning, whose father Archie spent his entire career as an NFL quarterback for a struggling New Orleans Saints team, let teams know where he preferred to play. "I don't care where I go," Roethlisberger said. "I don't care what they ask of me. I can't wait for draft day."[4]

2004 NFL DRAFT

Pick/Team/Player/College/Position

1. San Diego Chargers: Eli Manning, Mississippi, quarterback
2. Oakland Raiders: Robert Gallery, Iowa, offensive tackle
3. Arizona Cardinals: Larry Fitzgerald, Pittsburgh, wide receiver
4. New York Giants: Philip Rivers, North Carolina State, quarterback
5. Washington Redskins: Sean Taylor, Miami (Florida), safety
6. Cleveland Browns: Kellen Winslow Jr., Miami (Florida), tight end
7. Detroit Lions: Roy Williams, Texas, wide receiver
8. Atlanta Falcons: DeAngelo Hall, Virginia Tech, cornerback
9. Jacksonville Jaguars: Reggie Williams, Washington, wide receiver
10. Houston Texas: Dunta Robinson, South Carolina, cornerback
11. Pittsburgh Steelers: Ben Roethlisberger, Miami (Ohio), quarterback

DRAFT DAY ARRIVES

Roethlisberger and his family headed to New York City for the NFL Draft. Back in Oxford, Ohio, where Miami's campus is located, restaurants organized public gatherings to watch.

Roethlisberger arrived in a black suit and gold tie, coincidentally the same colors he would be wearing often for the Pittsburgh Steelers. But the attention was elsewhere throughout the day. The two other highly regarded quarterbacks were picked ahead of Roethlisberger—and were part of the day's most controversial story. The San Diego Chargers selected

EARLY PITTSBURGH STEELERS DRAFT PICKS

The Pittsburgh Steelers selected Roethlisberger with the eleventh overall pick in the 2004 NFL Draft. Because of the success of the franchise, high draft picks have been rare. They picked higher than eleventh just once between 1990 and 2008. Some of Pittsburgh's noteworthy top ten picks in the draft since 1950 include quarterback Len Dawson (fifth pick in 1957 from Purdue), defensive tackle "Mean" Joe Greene (fourth pick in 1969 from North Texas State), quarterback Terry Bradshaw (first pick in 1970 from Louisiana Tech), defensive back Rob Woodson (tenth pick in 1987 out of Purdue), and Plaxico Burress (eighth pick in 2000 out of Michigan State).

Manning with the first pick despite Manning saying he did not want to play for them. The New York Giants took Rivers with the fourth pick. The Giants and Chargers then traded the quarterbacks, with the Giants sending more draft picks to San Diego for the rights to Manning.

With those two quarterbacks gone and other teams looking to fill needs at other positions, Roethlisberger remained available longer than many had projected. The tension and anticipation continued until the Pittsburgh Steelers selected him with the eleventh pick of the draft.

Even Roethlisberger's press conference that day contained frequent mention of Manning and Rivers. "The attention has been on Eli all week and that's fine with me," Roethlisberger said. "I'm gonna let them get all the attention they want right now. When I start playing, that's when I'm going to be getting the attention."[5]

Only the highest regarded players are invited to wait for their names to be called at the draft. Roethlisberger was the last player left alone in the room. As the 2008 season approached, Ken Roethlisberger said the events of draft day were still driving his son more than four years later. "I think it motivated Ben more than anything else," Ken Roethlisberger said. "I think he fed off that."[6]

> "I'm gonna let them get all the attention they want right now. When I start playing, that's when I'm going to be getting the attention."
>
> —Ben Roethlisberger

The Steelers selected Roethlisberger with the eleventh pick in the NFL draft.

ROOKIE OF THE YEAR

Roethlisberger, like many rookie quarterbacks in the NFL, was ready to learn the professional game during practice and from the sideline on game days. His status suddenly changed when Pittsburgh quarterback Tommy Maddox was sidelined with an injury during the second game of the 2004 season.

Pittsburgh's experienced backup quarterback Charlie Batch suffered a knee injury in the preseason, so Roethlisberger was second on the Steelers' depth chart. When Maddox injured his right elbow against the Baltimore Ravens on the second weekend of the season, Roethlisberger stepped on the field. Instead of holding a clipboard on the sideline like most

COMFORTABLE TRANSITION

Roethlisberger said the adjustment to living in Pittsburgh, a city with a reputation of hard-working people who take extreme pride in their football team, was not too hard. "From what I can tell, Pittsburgh is almost like a bigger version of Findlay," Roethlisberger said of his hometown in Ohio. Roethlisberger described himself as a "Pittsburgh kind of guy" when explaining his preference for old-fashioned free weights over modern weight-lifting machines.

rookie quarterbacks, Roethlisberger now had to run the Steelers' offense.

TOUGH DEBUT

Roethlisberger's first pass was off the mark. His second was intercepted. The sudden, unplanned insertion in the lineup did not go well. Roethlisberger threw another interception, but did recover enough to throw 2 touchdown passes in the 30–13 loss.

The Steelers soon found that Maddox's injury was serious enough that he would miss the next week's game. Roethlisberger found himself preparing for his first professional start in the third game of his first season. He became the first rookie to start at quarterback for Pittsburgh since Bubby Brister eighteen years earlier. The Steelers found just enough

Roethlisberger talks with Tommy Maddox before the 2004 season.

offense to get through their first game with a rookie starting quarterback. Roethlisberger's 7-yard touchdown pass to Hines Ward clinched a 13–3 win against the Miami Dolphins. He threw just twenty-two times in the game, completing 12 passes for 163 yards.

Within weeks, Roethlisberger was not just helping the Steelers get by while Maddox was out. He was making a quick impression as one of the top young quarterbacks in pro football. Dallas Cowboys coach Bill

Parcells heaped praise on Roethlisberger before the rookie's fourth start. Some thought Parcells might just be following a coach's approach of building up an opponent. Parcells' motives may never be known, but Roethlisberger lived up to Parcells' descriptions as the best prospect he's seen in ten to fifteen years. "I have not seen anybody come into the league like that," Parcells said. "The only guy that I can say came in and in the first year started playing like he's been playing is Dan Marino."[1]

Roethlisberger led the Steelers to their fourth win in as many games when he connected on his first 7 passes and his last 11 against the Cowboys in a 24–20 victory. Dallas led 20–10 before Pittsburgh scored

NAME GAME

Roethlisberger is not the first famous person to have a sandwich named after him. In Roethlisberger's case, however, the name worked better than most. Brentwood Express, a restaurant on Saw Mill Boulevard in Pittsburgh, may have been the first to honor the Steelers quarterback with a menu item. It debuted a sandwich named the "Roethlis-burger", then adjusted the spelling to make it the "Roethlis-burgher."

The Brentwood Express was not alone. Among other sandwiches bearing the quarterback's name was "The Roethlisburger" at three Peppi's restaurants in the city. The $7 sandwich weighed in at 1 ½ pounds and featured ground beef, hot sausage, fried onions, scrambled egg, and American cheese.

two touchdowns in the final eleven minutes. Roethlisberger finished 21-for-25 for 193 yards and 2 touchdowns. He was establishing a routine of high-percentage, controlled passing that combined with Pittsburgh's strong defense and running game.

The performance against Dallas moved Roethlisberger up to fourth in the entire league in passing. He completed more than two-thirds of his passes in the game. There was no comparison among the highly regarded rookies. Eli Manning had made it off the bench just once. Philip Rivers had not played at all. Roethlisberger was already established as a successful NFL quarterback. "The thing that surprises me as a rookie in general is, number one, his composure under pressure," Steelers offensive coordinator Ken Whisenhunt said. "He also has good field vision, especially when he's on the move. And the third thing is he's smart with the ball. He doesn't make bad decisions."[2]

The media often talked of how Steelers coach Bill Cowher protected Roethlisberger by keeping him out of risky situations. This prevented the young quarterback from making lots of rookie mistakes. What was also clear, however, was that Roethlisberger's play allowed Pittsburgh to take advantage of its opportunities. The first thirteen times the Steelers crossed an opponent's 20-yard line with Roethlisberger at

Roethlisberger looks for an open receiver in a game against the Baltimore Ravens.

quarterback, they scored eleven touchdowns, including six on his passes and one on a Roethlisberger run. No team in the NFL was finding as much success in the "red zone."

Cowher disputed the notion that Roethlisberger had to be protected. "We haven't been conservative with him," Cowher said. "His decision-making has been excellent and the better it gets, the more you feel you can call things, that he is going to take what they give him. The coaches have done a great job of putting him in situations where we haven't asked him to do too much." But, Cowher said, Roethlisberger could make all the necessary plays when needed. "When we had to lean on him, he's made the plays. The more you are around him, the more you realize he is not just any ordinary rookie—that he is far more mature than his age."[3]

IN THE SPOTLIGHT

Roethlisberger often stayed out of the spotlight while competing at a smaller school like Miami. But within a year, he was the new center of attention in a football-crazy city and was entering the national spotlight. ESPN, *Sports Illustrated*, HBO, the *New York Times*, and the major broadcast networks lined up to tell Roethlisberger's story. The rookie's image to fans, teammates, and rivals would depend on how he handled the attention. "He's a very humble person who knows how important the team is around him," said Steelers publicist Ron Wahl, who was responsible for arranging many of the interviews. "He always compliments the team because he knows he couldn't do what he does without them."[4]

The Steelers could not have reached their levels of success without Roethlisberger's response to the challenge. Turning the team over to a rookie did not slow them down. Instead, Pittsburgh picked up momentum, putting together one of the most impressive winning streaks the league has ever seen. Pittsburgh won all thirteen games Roethlisberger started. He sat out the regular-season finale.

The public responded to what it saw. Black Steelers jerseys with Roethlisberger's name and number became the highest-selling jersey in the NFL.

FAMILIAR LOOK

Roethlisberger was playing on the highest level of football, but he was making the transition look relatively easy. Former teammates watched on television

DID YOU KNOW?

Roethlisberger, like every other NFL playoff participant, received a bonus for reaching the playoffs. Roethlisberger donated his entire $18,000 check to a tsunami relief fund.

and, to them, it looked as if Roethlisberger was making the same plays he had made in high school or college. Michael Larkin, who caught a pass from Roethlisberger in every game they played together in college, was still at Miami when his former quarterback was playing on Sundays. Larkin watched Steelers game tapes each Tuesday after practice and saw many similarities. When he saw Roethlisberger scramble on screen, Larkin assumed Steelers receivers were reading the play the same way he used to and knowing where to go with the extra time.

Larkin watched a high school tape with Mike Iriti, one of Roethlisberger's teammates at Findlay and Miami. "We were watching that and remembering all the things Ben did here at Miami," said Larkin, who was also Roethlisberger's college roommate. "Then, we're thinking that so far, in the NFL, it all looks the same. That's crazy. He made the same plays in high school and college that he's making now."[5]

NOBODY'S PERFECT

After beating Dallas, the Steelers had a week off before facing the defending Super Bowl champion New England Patriots. New England was on a twenty-one-game winning streak, counting the regular season and playoffs—the longest streak ever produced in the NFL. The streak came to an end when Roethlisberger completed 18 of 24 passes for 196 yards and 2 touchdowns in a 34–20 Pittsburgh

2004 PITTSBURGH STEELERS GAME-BY-GAME

REGULAR SEASON

9/12, OAKLAND	W, 24–21
9/19, at Baltimore	L, 13–30
9/26, at Miami	W, 13–3
10/3, CINCINNATI	W, 28–17
10/10, CLEVELAND	W, 34–23
10/17, at Dallas	W, 24–20
10/31, NEW ENGLAND	W, 34–20
11/7, PHILADELPHIA	W, 27–3
11/14, at Cleveland	W, 24–10
11/21, at Cincinnati	W, 19–14
11/28, WASHINGTON	W, 16–7
12/5, at Jacksonville	W, 17–16
12/12, NEW YORK JETS	W, 17–6
12/18, at New York Giants	W, 33–30
12/26, BALTIMORE	W, 20–7
1/2, at Buffalo	W, 29–24

PLAYOFFS

1/15, NEW YORK JETS	W, 20–17 (OT)
1/23, NEW ENGLAND	L, 27–41

victory. The win meant Pittsburgh was 6–1 and off to its best start in more than a quarter century since it started 7–0 in the 1978 season.

The Steelers made history a week later with the help of Roethlisberger's 2 touchdown passes.

The offense started strong—scoring the first three times it had the ball—and the defense shut down the unbeaten Philadelphia Eagles in a 27–3 victory. The wins represented the first time in NFL history that a team knocked off unbeaten opponents with at least six victories in back-to-back weeks.

REVISITING THE DRAFT

The Steelers record improved to 12–1 and their status as a playoff team was no longer in doubt. Roethlisberger, however, still had plenty of reason to be motivated for the team's fourteenth game. Pittsburgh was headed for the Meadowlands in New Jersey to play the New York Giants. The Giants picked quarterback Philip Rivers with the fourth selection and traded him to get Manning, who had been selected first by the San Diego Chargers. The Giants and Chargers needed to find the best quarterbacks and thought they found them elsewhere. This played a large part in Roethlisberger slipping down to the eleventh pick in the draft. "He is playing with

PRIME TIME

The Steelers struggled in the 2003 season. That meant less time in the spotlight during the 2004 season. In its only prime-time game of the year, Pittsburgh defeated Jacksonville 17–16 on a Sunday night in December. The Steelers were down two points and out of timeouts when Roethlisberger led them down the field, covering 56 yards in six plays to set up Jeff Reed's game-winning, 37-yard field goal with eighteen seconds left.

a chip because of that," Steelers wide receiver Plaxico Burress said. "I mean, he's the best quarterback in the draft, but they were saying he's not."[6]

Roethlisberger admitted that the draft might have played a role in motivating him at times during his rookie season. He acknowledged the "chip on his shoulder," but said it was only a component, along with the general will to win. "When there are doubters, it always fuels the fire a little bit," he said. "When people say you can't do something, if you are a competitor it drives you."[7]

The Steelers were no longer relying on defense on December 18, 2004. Roethlisberger and Manning turned the game into an offensive show. Manning, who had just 1 touchdown pass and 6 interceptions while losing his first four starts, came up with his first strong game as a professional with 16 completions in 23 attempts and 2 touchdowns. Roethlisberger topped Manning's yardage output with a season-high 316 on 18-for-28 passing. After the Giants moved ahead with 8:15 left, a 36-yard pass from Roethlisberger to Antwaan Randle El helped set up a game-winning, 1-yard touchdown run by Jerome Bettis to give the Steelers a 33–30 victory.

> "When people say you can't do something, if you are a competitor it drives you."
>
> —Ben Roethlisberger

BIG FINISH

The Steelers never lost their momentum in the 2004 regular season. A year after struggling to a 6–10 finish, they went 15–1 and won the AFC Central, finishing six games in front of the Baltimore Ravens. As the season neared its conclusion, there was no longer any question of whether Maddox would take his job back. Instead, the veteran quarterback was there to help guide Roethlisberger through the season, offering advice during games. "He'll meet me halfway out on the field to answer a question for me," Roethlisberger said. "I owe so much of my success to his help."[8]

The thirteen straight wins with Roethlisberger at quarterback were the most ever with a rookie leading the way. It helped him make history in another way, too. Roethlisberger was the first quarterback to win the Associated Press Rookie of the Year award since it began in 1957. Roethlisberger finished fifth in the NFL's complex passer rating formula, behind only Peyton Manning, Daunte Culpepper, Drew Brees, and Donovan McNabb.

PLAYOFFS

Although the Steelers made a drastic improvement and at 15–1 had the best record in the league—better than the Patriots (14–2) and Eagles (13–3)—they appeared not quite ready for a championship run.

ROOKIE QUARTERBACKS IN THE PLAYOFFS

Roethlisberger became the eighth rookie quarterback to start a playoff game since the NFL merged with the American Football League in 1970. Only three other quarterbacks won their first game—Pat Haden in 1976, Dieter Brock in 1985, and Shaun King in 1999.

The playoffs became a struggle. Roethlisberger's 2 interceptions in the divisional playoffs against the New York Jets nearly cost them a win. One was returned for a touchdown. The other, with 2:03 left in the fourth quarter, helped set up a chance at a game-winning field goal for the Jets. Doug Brien missed that chance and the teams went to overtime. With a second chance, Roethlisberger drove the Steelers down the field to set up Jeff Reed's 33-yard field goal for a 20–17 win.

New England ended Pittsburgh's season the next week on its way to a second straight Super Bowl victory. The Patriots opened a 21-point lead in the first half and intercepted Roethlisberger three times in a 41–27 victory. In the NFC Championship Game, Philadelphia beat the Atlanta Falcons 27–10. The all-Pennsylvania Super Bowl that Keystone state fans hoped for did not materialize.

6 ROAD TO THE SUPER BOWL

The following year, the Pittsburgh Steelers barely made the playoffs, sneaking in as the sixth seed in the AFC. But they were on the verge of winning their second-round game against the Indianapolis Colts, a team that looked invincible while starting the season 13–0. The Steelers had an eleven-point lead at one point during the fourth quarter, but now it was down to three. With a little more than a minute remaining in the game, Pittsburgh stopped Indianapolis and its dangerous quarterback Peyton Manning on a fourth down. Now the Steelers just needed to run the remaining time off the clock.

Clinging to a 21–18 lead, Pittsburgh took over at the Indianapolis 2-yard line with 1:20 left to play.

Roethlisberger handed off to Jerome Bettis. Normally, Roethlisberger's work would be done. On this play, it was only beginning. The Steelers would have been thrilled with a touchdown when Bettis started his run, but really they just needed to run some time off the clock. The Steelers would not get either.

Indianapolis linebacker Gary Brackett hit Bettis, forcing a fumble. Then Colts' defensive back Nick Harper picked it up. Suddenly, Harper was heading in the other direction, making cuts and threatening to take the ball all 98 yards for a touchdown. If he made it to the end zone, the Colts would take the lead with about one minute left to play.

That is when Roethlisberger re-entered the picture. The quarterback never gave up on chasing Harper. When Harper tried to cut to his left past Roethlisberger, the quarterback reached out and got

DID YOU KNOW?

When Pittsburgh beat Indianapolis 21–18 during the 2005–06 playoffs, it was the first time in franchise history that the Steelers had won back-to-back road playoff games. A week later the Steelers beat the Denver Broncos 34–17 to advance to the Super Bowl with three straight road wins.

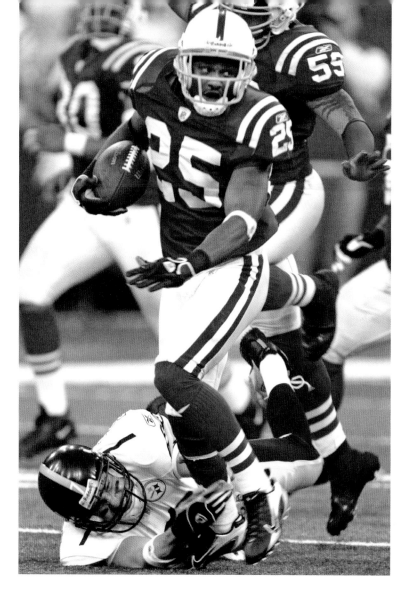

Roethlisberger tackles the Colts' Nick Harper, preventing a touchdown.

a hand on Harper's right leg. It was just enough to send Harper tumbling to the ground at the Indianapolis 42, well short of a touchdown.

Roethlisberger's tackle saved the Steelers from falling behind and kept their hopes alive for a spot in the AFC Championship game. "Once in a blue moon, Jerome fumbles," Roethlisberger said. "Once in a blue moon, I make a tackle. They just happened to be in the same game."[1]

When the Colts' offense took the field, Manning moved Indianapolis inside the Pittsburgh 30 and kicker Mike Vanderjagt lined up for a 46-yard field goal. If he made it, the game would likely go into overtime. But Vanderjagt's kick sailed wide right. The Steelers moved on. With two more wins, the Steelers would soon be celebrating the franchise's fifth Super Bowl championship three weeks later.

"It was a unique game," Bettis said. "It ranks right up there. It was crazy."[2] The Steelers, the first sixth-seeded team to reach the AFC Championship game, would never have made it through the game without their young quarterback saving them. "It went from an all-time high to an all-time low, back to an all-time high," Steelers wide receiver Hines Ward said.[3]

> It went from an all-time high to an all-time low, back to an all-time high.
>
> —Jerome Bettis

EXTENDING THE STREAK

The road to the Super Bowl was not an easy one. Roethlisberger was a winner in his first fifteen regular-season starts at quarterback, including the

THE PERFECT GAMES

The NFL uses a complex mathematical ratings system—combining completion percentage, average gain per attempt, touchdown percentage, and interception percentage—to rank its passers. The maximum rating in the system is 158.3.

Roethlisberger hit the maximum rating in the first game of the 2005 season when he completed 9 of 11 passes for 218 yards and 2 touchdowns in a 34–7 win over Tennessee. He was the thirty-second quarterback in league history to have a passing game rated at 158.3. Roethlisberger added two more perfect games in passing rating during the 2007 season, on November 15 against Baltimore and December 20 at St. Louis.

first two games of the 2005 season. The Steelers—and their quarterback—made it look easy. Roethlisberger was needed for just eleven passes in the season-opening 34–7 romp over Tennessee. It was the fewest times Pittsburgh threw the ball since the 1977 season. The following week, Roethlisberger connected on two-thirds of his passes, including completions of 36, 54, and 40 yards in a 27–7 win over Houston. In the two games, Roethlisberger was 23-for-32 for 472 yards and 4 touchdowns.

Injuries forced Roethlisberger to miss four games in 2005.

The streak, as well as the high completion percentage, disappeared the following week against the Patriots. Roethlisberger completed less than half of his passes. But he came back from a shoulder injury to lead the team down the field on a late scoring drive that finished with a touchdown pass to Ward. It forced a 20–20 tie with New England. The Patriots came back down the field, however, and scored a field goal to win 23–20.

INJURIES

Roethlisberger's first chance to start in the NFL came from an injury to a teammate. Now he was on the other end of the injury problems that strike pro football players as a whole and quarterbacks in particular. After coming back and playing through a sore shoulder early in the season, Roethlisberger suffered a hyperextended left knee in the Steelers' fifth game of the season at San Diego. He was leading the

2005 PITTSBURGH STEELERS GAME-BY-GAME

REGULAR SEASON

9/11, TENNESSEE	W, 34–7
9/18, at Houston	W, 27–7
9/25, NEW ENGLAND	L, 20–23
10/10, at San Diego	W, 24–22
10/16, JACKSONVILLE	L, 17–23 (OT)
10/23, at Cincinnati	W, 27–13
10/31, BALTIMORE	W, 20–19
11/6, at Green Bay	W, 20–10
11/13, CLEVELAND	W, 34–21
11/20, at Baltimore	L, 13–16 (OT)
11/28, at Indianapolis	L, 7–26
12/4, CINCINNATI	L, 31–38
12/11, CHICAGO	W, 21–9
12/18, at Minnesota	W, 18–3
12/24, at Cleveland	W, 41–0
1/1, DETROIT	W, 35–21

PLAYOFFS

1/8, at Cincinnati	W, 31–17
1/15, at Indianapolis	W, 21–18
1/22, at Denver	W, 34–17

SUPER BOWL

2/5, Seattle	W, 21–10

Steelers to a come-from-behind victory when it happened. Roethlisberger sat out the next game against Jacksonville.

Roethlisberger was back after missing just one full game. For the first time in nineteen starts as a pro, he was called on to throw 30 passes against Baltimore on Halloween night. The game was his last until the end of November. A torn meniscus in his right knee forced Roethlisberger out of the lineup for three straight games. He returned the weekend after Thanksgiving to play in a game at Indianapolis.

Back from his injuries, it was time for Roethlisberger to make a late push to help Pittsburgh get into the playoffs. He opened December with what was then the busiest passing day of his pro career. Roethlisberger threw the ball 41 times, completing 29 for 386 yards and 3 touchdowns in a 38–31 loss to Cincinnati. With wins in the final four games, Roethlisberger improved his two-year record as a starter to 22–3 and led the Steelers to the playoffs with an 11–5 record.

Roethlisberger finished the season with 17 touchdown passes and just 9 interceptions. He was the third-ranked passer in the NFL.

POSTSEASON

The road to the Super Bowl started on January 8, 2006, in Cincinnati, Ohio, with a brilliant performance by Roethlisberger. The AFC Central

Division champion Bengals opened leads of 10–0 and 17–7, but Roethlisberger's most efficient playoff performance brought the Steelers back. He completed 14 of his 19 passes for 208 yards and 3 touchdowns in a 31–17 victory.

The Steelers came out passing against Indianapolis, throwing on seven of the first ten plays. Roethlisberger was sharp early, leading the Steelers to two touchdowns in their first three possessions. After his game-saving tackle allowed the Steelers to hold on against the Colts, Roethlisberger had another big effort in the AFC Championship Game win at Denver. He completed 21 of 29 passes for 275 yards and 2 touchdowns while also running for a score.

Just as his tackling helped get the Steelers to the Super Bowl, Roethlisberger found other unconventional quarterback methods while contributing to the championship. On a day when the quarterback struggled to connect with his receivers, Roethlisberger made a key block to clear the way for Antwaan Randle El's 43-yard touchdown pass to Ward in the 21–10 victory over the Seattle Seahawks in the Super Bowl.

DID YOU KNOW?

Roethlisberger was the first quarterback in NFL history to lead his team to the conference championship game in each of his first two seasons in the league.

Roethlisberger waves to the crowd in downtown Pittsburgh during the Steelers' Super Bowl parade.

7

INJURY AND ILLNESS

Ben Roethlisberger was driving through Pittsburgh on his 2005 Suzuki motorcycle the morning of June 12, 2006. As he arrived at an intersection, a car approaching from the opposite direction made a left turn. Roethlisberger's motorcycle collided with the silver Chrysler New Yorker. The impact from the crash sent Roethlisberger flying into the car's windshield. When he bounced off, Roethlisberger's head, which was not protected by a helmet, smacked the pavement first. Blood pooled around him as onlookers gathered to check on him.

Just months after becoming a Super Bowl champion, Roethlisberger's career—and briefly, his life—were in jeopardy. He lay on the ground, bleed-

HELMETS

Helmets were mandatory when riding motorcycles in Pennsylvania for thirty-five years until state laws were amended in 2003, making helmets optional under certain circumstances. For example, motorcyclists who were twenty-one years of age or older, who had a license for two or more years, or who had completed safety training had the option of riding without a helmet.

ing from several wounds to his head and face. Word that the famous football player was being rushed to a city hospital spread quickly—too quickly for some family members.

UNCERTAINTY

Carlee Roethlisberger, Ben's sister, was enjoying a special time in her own athletic career. A day earlier, she had committed to play basketball at the University of Oklahoma on an athletics scholarship. As she prepared for an Amateur Athletic Union basketball game, her cell phone rang in the locker room. A friend was on the other line asking about a report of the motorcycle accident she had seen on ESPN. It was the first Carlee heard about the accident and left her in need of more information. "She said it was on ESPN and he was on his way to the hospital," Carlee

Police examine Roethlisberger's wrecked motorcycle.

Roethlisberger said of her friend's call. "I ran into the gym looking for my dad and I couldn't find him right away. It was crazy."[1]

Ken and Carlee Roethlisberger left the game in Cincinnati and started driving to Pittsburgh. They listened to radio news reports, speculation, and

PLAYING IT SAFE

Cleveland Browns tight end Kellen Winslow Jr. suffered a major knee injury in a motorcycle accident that caused him to miss the entire 2005 season. After that, Pittsburgh Steelers coach Bill Cowher had a talk with Roethlisberger, who also enjoyed riding motorcycles. "He talked about being a risk-taker and I'm not really a risk-taker," Roethlisberger said. "I'm pretty conservative and laid back, but the big thing is to be careful. I'll just continue to be careful."

When Roethlisberger decided not to give up his hobby, Terry Bradshaw, the Hall of Fame quarterback who led the Steelers to their first four Super Bowl titles, let his opinion be known during a visit to 2005 training camp. "Ride it when you retire," Bradshaw said.

commentary along the way. Carlee later described the 283-mile (455 km) drive as the longest trip of her life. Media arrived at the Roethlisberger home and watched as Brenda Roethlisberger packed the car and headed for Pittsburgh herself.

While family was driving in from Ohio, members of the Steelers organization were arriving at Mercy Hospital. In the time immediately after Roethlisberger made it to the hospital, there was some uncertainty about his condition. When Ken and Carlee made it past media inquiries upon their arrival at the hospital, information was hard to find. "It was scary," Carlee said. "We couldn't see him right away because he was in surgery."[2]

The surgery lasted seven hours. Doctors worked on injuries that included multiple cuts, a broken jaw, a broken nose, and a broken orbital bone. One of the cuts on the back of his head was nine inches long. Along with the broken jaw, Roethlisberger lost two teeth and chipped many others. Once the bleeding from the various cuts was under control, Roethlisberger's condition became less dangerous. The surgery involved the placement of many small titanium plates and screws to repair Roethlisberger's face. "He suffered multiple facial fractures," Dr. Daniel Pituch, chief of oral and maxillofacial surgery at Mercy Hospital, said in a late-night press conference following the completion of surgery. "All of the fractures were successfully repaired. His brain, spine, chest, and abdomen appear to be without serious injury. And there are no other confirmed injuries at this time."[3]

Roethlisberger's family requested the hospital limit comments on the injury other than the press

FEELING FORTUNATE

Saying he was "fortunate to be alive," Roethlisberger apologized to fans and said he would wear a helmet if riding a motorcycle in the future. In a June 16, 2006, press release, three days after his scary accident in downtown Pittsburgh, Roethlisberger said: "In the past few days, I've gained a new perspective on life." Roethlisberger acknowledged in the press release that he had a responsibility to protect his health in the offseason in order to remain healthy to lead the team.

conference. But ESPN did report that Roethlisberger also had minor injuries to his knees from hitting the pavement. Dr. Larry Jones, chief of trauma at Mercy Hospital, reported during the press conference that following surgery, Roethlisberger was coherent and aware of what had happened. He was officially listed in "serious but stable condition" the first night in the hospital.

MORE HEALTH ISSUES

The broken jaw and other injuries healed in time for Roethlisberger to begin preparation for his third NFL season in the late summer of 2006. To some observers, Roethlisberger looked sharper in training camp than he had a year earlier when the Steelers were starting out the Super Bowl championship season.

Just when Roethlisberger seemed ready to start the season, another unexpected health issue arose. He was feeling ill when he reported to the Steelers practice facility the Sunday morning prior to a game. A team doctor examined Roethlisberger and sent him to the hospital for emergency surgery to remove his appendix.

The setback was a disappointment to Roethlisberger's teammates. "All he did to come back," guard Alan Faneca said. "He's had a busy offseason and preseason."[4] It was immediately obvious that Roethlisberger would miss the Thursday night game

LAPAROSCOPIC APPENDECTOMY

Roethlisberger underwent a laparoscopic appendectomy days before the start of the 2006 NFL season. Laparoscopic surgery involves the insertion of cameras and surgical instruments through small incisions. An appendix can be removed through one of those small incisions. By avoiding larger incisions, patients spend less time in the hospital and have a faster recovery.

that kicked off the entire NFL season. Missing the second, and even third, game also seemed possible.

A SEASON OF STRUGGLES

Roethlisberger's quick return was surprising to some. He started Pittsburgh's second game, just fifteen days after surgery. Although he got back quickly from both injury and illness, there were some signs that there were lingering effects on Roethlisberger. The first outing was a tough one with just 141 yards and 17 completions on 32 attempts against Jacksonville. The next two games were not much better. But Roethlisberger broke loose against Kansas City and hit 16 of 19 passes for 238 yards and his first 2 touchdown passes of the season. The 45–7 rout of the Chiefs ended a three-game losing streak and was the first time in the season that the Steelers won with their starting quarterback in the lineup.

Roethlisberger and the Steelers didn't have the best season in 2006.

Once again, Roethlisberger was seemingly headed in the right direction when physical problems became a factor. He followed up the Kansas City game with the best first half of his career when he completed 15 of 20 passes for 235 yards and 3 touch-downs against Atlanta. He had to come out of the game after being hit in the head by Atlanta's Chauncey Davis. While Roethlisberger sat out with a concussion, the Steelers lost in overtime, 41–38.

A 301-yard passing day against Oakland followed. Then he threw a team-record 38 completions against Denver, when he turned his 54 attempts into 433 yards. The only time a Steelers quarterback ever threw for more yards was when Tommy Maddox threw for 473 in a 2002 game. The extra passing, however, was a sign that the Steelers were not able to succeed with their usual game plan. They lost both games.

Even in times of struggle, Roethlisberger added to the big-yardage games by showing the ability to come through in the fourth quarter. After the Steelers scored just three points for three quarters, Roethlisberger rallied them to a 24–20 win at Cleveland in November. He scrambled away from a sack to hit wide receiver Santonio Holmes on a 20-yard touchdown pass and then threw the game-winner to Willie Parker from 4 yards out.

The Steelers improved from 2–6 in the first half of the season to 6–2 in the second half, but an 8–8 finish was not enough for the defending Super Bowl champions to get back to the playoffs. "It was tough, frustrating," Roethlisberger said. "At least you know it will be awfully hard for next year to be any worse. We're going to get better."[5]

When the season was over, Roethlisberger had 18 touchdowns and 23 interceptions. It was the only time in the first five years of his career that he threw more interceptions than touchdowns. He did pass for a career-high total of 3,513 yards.

> "At least you know it will be awfully hard for next year to be any worse. We're going to get better."
>
> —Ben Roethlisberger

"I told some of the receivers, and some of the other guys, that we need to get better," Roethlisberger said. "We know that. We feel we've made big steps with the young guys that we have, and we'll get better this offseason."[6]

8 BUILDING A FOUNDATION

The police department in Findlay, Ohio, found itself in need when Flip, its only police dog, was shot in 2006. Flip had wandered away from the home where he lived with officer Byron Deeter. A neighbor, Steven E. Vanderhoff, told police that he arrived home and saw Flip on his property. Vanderhoff, who had his young son in the car, said he went into the house, got a gun, and shot Flip when he would not leave Vanderhoff's yard.

Ben Roethlisberger is a dog lover and had started a charitable foundation early in his professional career. He saw a situation where he could help. The Steelers quarterback pledged to provide a replacement for Flip. Not only did Roethlisberger make sure that Findlay was able to get a new dog, Spike, he also decided to become more involved with police dogs in general. The Ben Roethlisberger Foundation now assists police and fire departments with obtaining service dogs.

Spike, a fifty-five-pound (24.9 kg) Belgian Malinois, was less than two years old at the time. He joined Deeter on loan the day after the shooting. With Roethlisberger's help, arrangements were made for Spike to be able to replace Flip. "I always had dogs around my house, and my dad instilled in me a love and respect for animals," Roethlisberger wrote in a *USA Weekend Magazine* story. "Today, I have two wonderful dogs to come home to every day."[1]

Because of The Ben Roethlisberger Foundation, many more police departments have a dog they can

MAN'S BEST FRIEND

Roethlisberger grew up in a house where there was always a dog as a family pet. Brandy, a golden retriever, was the first dog he can recall from his childhood. It only made sense that when Roethlisberger moved to Pittsburgh on his own that he would need a dog. "As soon as I moved to Pittsburgh, I got Zeus from a breeder in Germany," Roethlisberger said. The rottweiler eventually had to share space in the house. The Swiss government invited the Roethlisberger family there to explore their heritage and presented Ben with Hercules, who he says is now a 110-pound (44.9 kg) lap dog. "They get along fine," Roethlisberger said. "They jostle each other going up the stairs, just like children."

RESPECTING AUTHORITY

Before Roethlisberger began his pursuit of a pro football career, he thought he might want to become an FBI agent. When he watched movies as a kid, Ben thought being a spy like James Bond would be fun.

Donating dogs through the Ben Roethlisberger Foundation gave him a chance to have a connection to many police departments. "I have a lot of friends, both in my hometown and in Pittsburgh, who are officers, so I try to show my support in any way possible," Roethlisberger said.

rely on. Deeter said the animals can be invaluable on the job, but it is difficult to always define where they have helped. "How many times did someone not fight with me because they knew the dog was there?" Deeter asked. "How many times did someone not run because they knew the dog was there? You don't know what behavior the dog has deterred."[2]

Police dogs are trained in tasks such as sniffing for bombs or illegal drugs. They are often helpful in assisting in crowd control. "Unfortunately, I'm not able to meet most of the dogs our grants provide, but I have played with Spike, Flip's successor," Roethlisberger said. "He is an amazing animal and can jump right up to the ceiling of an office building—like eight feet."[3]

The Ben Roethlisberger Foundation already had other projects. It was funding a youth football program in Findlay and providing benefits to the Ronald McDonald House in Pittsburgh. The foundation committed to providing grants to buy a police or fire dog in each city where the Steelers played in 2007, with one dog being provided in or around Pittsburgh for each of the eight weeks the Steelers were home. If a city did not need a dog, the foundation provided bulletproof vests for the animals, something that was often not a part of a police department budget.

Roethlisberger kept the program going. In 2008, the Giving Back Fund helped manage an application process for the cities in each metropolitan market where the Steelers played. The Giving Back Fund is an organization that helps many athletes and celebrities manage their charitable foundations.

THE GIVING BACK FUND

The Giving Back Fund was founded in 1997 as a philanthropic resource for the sports and entertainment communities. Roethlisberger, basketball players Jalen Rose and Elton Brand, actress Jamie-Lynn Sigler, and singer Justin Timberlake are among those who have worked with the Giving Back Fund. The fund provides services to those interested in giving back to their community.

Roethlisberger jokes with teammates during warmups for Super Bowl XLIII.

The trained dogs generally cost between $11,000 and $12,000.

Roethlisberger took pride in bringing "that love and respect" for animals from his childhood into his adult life. "This is a good way to combine that passion with a desire to support the police and fire departments, which deserve all the appropriate resources needed to protect our cities and neighborhoods, and allow these brave men and women to arrive home safely," he said.[4]

HELPING OTHERS

When Roethlisberger created his foundation, there was not a definite plan on what would become the largest projects. Instead there was just a general sense of trying to offer help. "I was raised to appreciate my blessings and always try to help others not as fortunate as myself," he said.[5] Ken Roethlisberger, Ben's father, runs the foundation. Marathon Oil partnered with the foundation and WFIN-AM radio to support Findlay youth football. Marathon pledged $1,000 to the foundation for every touchdown run or pass by Roethlisberger in the 2007 season. The pledge was specifically for the development of a football complex. Roethlisberger then went out

> **I was raised to appreciate my blessings and always try to help others not as fortunate as myself.**
>
> —Ben Roethlisberger

MAKE A WISH

Akeem Havens, a paralyzed fourteen-year-old boy from Georgia, had his dream come true on May 29, 2008. He got to spend a day with Roethlisberger and the Pittsburgh Steelers at team headquarters. The visit was arranged by the Make-A-Wish Foundation, which arranges for dreams to come true for children with life-threatening medical conditions. "It's just one of the best things I've done," said Havens, who suffered from paralysis and kidney failure following an accident when he was seven years old, "probably one of the funnest days of my life."

Roethlisberger signs autographs while competing in a celebrity pro-am golf tournament in 2005.

and threw 4 touchdown passes in the first week of the promotion to get the fundraising started.

His goal of helping others was fulfilled with the foundation. But Roethlisberger also helped in other charitable areas that were not always directly tied to his foundation.

One example was Roethlisberger serving as the featured celebrity golfer at the Tenth annual Sheetz Family Charities For the Kids Golf Classic in Williamsburg, Virginia, in June 2008. The tournament raises money to buy clothing and presents for kids at Christmastime and to make donations to the Make-A-Wish Foundation.

BACK IN FORM

Hines Ward, the Steelers' leader in receptions, was already out with a knee injury as the team prepared to host the Seattle Seahawks October 8, 2007. It was a rematch of the Super Bowl less than two years earlier. During pregame warm-ups, wide receiver Santonio Holmes, the team leader in receiving yards, strained his hamstring.

With little notice, the Steelers now had to take the field without either of Roethlisberger's two established receiving threats. When the Seahawks saw that Holmes was also not playing and the Steelers were down to only three healthy wide receivers, they were well aware that Pittsburgh needed to run the ball often. The Seahawks adjusted their defense accordingly.

The Steelers now had reasons to expect running and passing the ball to be much tougher. Pittsburgh's defense came through with the kind of effort for which the franchise has become known. The offensive line handled the new challenges it faced. And Roethlisberger turned in one of the most impressive performances of his career, putting together a strong statistical game in difficult circumstances.

Roethlisberger completed his final 13 passes to finish 18-for-22 for 206 yards and a touchdown. He appropriately shared credit when it was over. But his leadership of an offense stripped of its most dangerous weapons was a big factor in a 21–0 win. "You've got to give the line a lot of credit," Roethlisberger said. "They gave me a lot of time and the receivers got open."[1]

One of the reasons Seattle did not score was that when the Seahawks gave up the ball, Roethlisberger made sure they waited before getting it back. His passes and scrambles helped Pittsburgh hold the ball for more than twenty-four of the thirty minutes in the second half.

BETTER THAN EVER

Performances like the one against Seattle became almost routine for Roethlisberger during the 2007 season. Not only did he bounce back from the disappointment of the injury- and illness-plagued 2006 season, but he came back an even better quarterback than he had been in his first two seasons as a professional.

When the season started, Roethlisberger was considered by many analysts to be around the middle of the pack among NFL starting quarterbacks. Being one of the fifteen or so best in the world at what you do is hardly cause for disappointment, but Roethlisberger was about to prove he deserved more consideration. Throughout the season, Roethlisberger was statistically second best in passing. Only New England's Tom Brady was better. He also ranked as the second-best runner among quarterbacks behind only Tennessee's Vince Young.

The season went well right from the start. Roethlisberger threw just 23 passes on opening day and his other numbers were average, but 4 of those passes went for touchdowns in a 34–7 romp over the

2007 NFL PASSING LEADERS

QUARTERBACK	COM	ATT	PCT	YDS	TD	INT	RAT
1. Tom Brady, New England	398	578	68.9	4608	50	8	117.2
2. Ben Roethlisberger, Pittsburgh	264	404	65.3	3154	32	11	104.1
3. David Garrard, Jacksonville	208	325	64.0	2509	18	3	102.2
4. Peyton Manning, Indianapolis	337	515	65.4	4040	31	14	98.0
5. Tony Romo, Dallas	335	520	64.4	4211	36	19	97.4

New coach Mike Tomlin brought a more encouraging coaching style to the Steelers.

Cleveland Browns. "It makes all the hard work put in this offseason feel good so far," Roethlisberger said.[2]

With new coach Mike Tomlin and new offensive coordinator Bruce Arians, the Steelers showed off a new style offensively. They mixed formations more, switching to as many as four wide receivers at a time or replacing them and putting up to three tight ends together. Roethlisberger looked comfortable from the start, beginning a new working relationship on a positive note. "We've been talking about it all offseason, being able to finally utilize the weapons we have at receiver," Roethlisberger said. "I feel like we were very unpredictable for the defense."[3]

ESTABLISHING CONTROL

Mike Tomlin took over for Steelers' fifteen-year coach Bill Cowher prior to the 2007 season. Replacing a powerful and respected figure in Cowher, Tomlin immediately established his authority. "He came in and was tough on us," Roethlisberger said. "He didn't give us much time off. We were so used to one way, with the time schedules and this and that. The change kind of made some guys grumpy at times. But guys understood what he was doing." Roethlisberger said it was not long before the team was excited about playing for its new coach. "I think guys have really taken the new coach well," he said. "There's kind of a new interest and excitement, and level of wanting to win for this coach."

A MATTER OF TRUST

Tomlin said he had confidence that Roethlisberger was ready for a big season. Despite his young age, he had already been through a career's worth of experiences. Roethlisberger had been thrust into the starting lineup unexpectedly, led his team to the Super Bowl, and had physical problems complicate a season. "He's seen about everything that this profession has to offer," Tomlin said. "That creates a maturity in him that you can't manufacture in a twenty-five-year-old guy."[4]

Everything the profession has to offer included a coaching change, which Roethlisberger adapted to well. Roethlisberger described Bill Cowher as a Hall of Fame coach who made him a better player. But he also said Cowher could be intimidating at times. He said Tomlin addresses mistakes differently, that he "wants to talk to you about it or encourage you— 'You're going to be OK'—whereas Cowher would yell at you or scream at you."[5]

Just as Cowher and Tomlin had differences, former offensive coordinator Ken Whisenhunt and Arians had differences. Roethlisberger's assignment had been to run the offense that Whisenhunt designed and execute the game plan Whisenhunt formulated. Arians wanted Roethlisberger to help create the playbook and game plan so that he knew his quarterback was confident in the offense he was running. "It feels great to know your coaches

have trust in you and will sit down and talk to you," Roethlisberger said.[6] Instead of receiving the game plan on Wednesday mornings at the Steelers practice facility, Roethlisberger was discussing it with Arians on Monday and Tuesday and received a draft copy by fax at home on Tuesday nights.

Running back Jerome Bettis, a veteran leader of the first two teams Roethlisberger played on, was a television analyst for NBC during the 2007 season. He could see the changes in his former teammate. "When we got him, he was a young guy thrust onto a veteran team, and he was given a pretty short leash," Bettis said. "But the new staff has given him more of the reins. He's been given input; it gives you ownership. You can see that carry over to the way he plays."[7]

ADDING IT UP

The changes produced many positive results. They were a hint of even better times ahead. The Steelers won their first three games by a total score of 97–26. They reached mid-November with a 7–2 record with the first four wins coming by a minimum of three touchdowns and only one coming by fewer than eleven points. That one close win was a 31–28 victory over Cleveland, giving the Steelers a season sweep of their home-and-home series with the Browns.

Roethlisberger threw a career high 32 touchdowns in 2007.

"DON'T QUIT"

Terry Hoeppner, Roethlisberger's college coach at Miami University of Ohio, died of complications from a brain tumor June 19, 2007. When a *Sports Illustrated* reporter visited with Roethlisberger during the 2007 season, it was clear that Hoeppner's influence was still all around the Pittsburgh Steelers quarterback.

A poem titled "Don't Quit" can be found in a frame above Roethlisberger's desk at home, folded up in the console of his car as well as laminated and posted inside his locker. Hoeppner shared the poem many times with his Miami players. He and Roethlisberger later read it in each other's hospital rooms when Roethlisberger was recovering from his motorcycle accident and when Hoeppner was battling his brain tumor.

A portion of the poem reads:

> *Success is failure turned inside out;*
> *The silver tint of the clouds of doubt;*
> *And you never can tell how*
> *close you are,*
> *It may be near when it seems afar,*
> *So stick to the fight when you're*
> *hardest hit;*
> *It's when things seem worst*
> *that you mustn't quit*[9]

PRIME TIME

Roethlisberger had a record-tying performance on Monday Night Football on November 5, 2007. In the Steelers' 38–7 rout of the Baltimore Ravens, Roethlisberger needed just 16 attempts to throw 5 touchdown passes. That tied a Monday Night record as well as the Steelers team record shared already by Terry Bradshaw and Mark Malone. Bradshaw was at Heinz Field that night as part of the Steelers seventy-fifth anniversary all-time team celebration.

It ultimately decided the AFC North Division title when both teams finished with 10–6 records.

The Steelers lost some of their momentum heading into the playoffs. After dropping games to New England and Jacksonville, they beat the St. Louis Rams, 41–24. Pittsburgh was 10–5 with at least one touchdown pass from Roethlisberger in all but one game. The quarterback was one of the many key players to rest in the final game of the regular season, a 27–21 loss to the Baltimore Ravens.

Roethlisberger threw a team-record 32 touchdown passes in 2007. He was chosen to play in the Pro Bowl, the NFL's all-star game, for the first time in his four-year career.

IMPORTANT COMEBACK

Pittsburgh trailed the Cleveland Browns, 21–9, at halftime on November 11. The game wound up being the most important game of the Steelers' 2007 season. After starting 2–3, the Browns won eight of their final eleven games to catch the Steelers in the standings. But one of those losses was November 11, when the Steelers came back. The Steelers clinched a tiebreaker advantage that would award them the AFC North championship.

PLAYOFF LOSS

The 2007 season came to an abrupt end in Pittsburgh's first playoff game when the Steelers fell behind by eighteen points before rallying in a 31–29 loss to Jacksonville. The Steelers scored nineteen straight points in the fourth quarter to take a 29–28 lead before losing on a field goal.

Roethlisberger built up career playoff highs in attempts (42), completions (29), and passing yards (337) while throwing 2 touchdowns and 3 costly interceptions. "He messed it up in the first half, and a lot of time people go in the tank, but he brought us back, made plays to win the ballgame," Arians said.[8] The Steelers did not get that playoff win, but they were ready by the next time they got to the playoffs.

SECOND CHANCE

Roethlisberger got a second chance to be first. When the Steelers followed up the 2008 NFL regular season by advancing to Super Bowl XLIII, Roethlisberger was back on the football's ultimate stage. Just three years earlier, he had become the youngest person ever to be the winning starting quarterback in a Super Bowl.

Roethlisberger, however, carried around the knowledge that he really had not played up to his personal standards the first time around. He made some key plays and certainly showed his physical toughness, but it had not been one of those classic performances that made previous Super Bowl-winning quarterbacks into legends.

MOST PLAYOFF, SUPER BOWL WINS BY QUARTERBACK IN FIRST FIVE SEASONS IN NFL

QUARTERBACK	PLAYOFF WINS	SUPER BOWL WINS
1. Tom Brady	9	3
2. Ben Roethlisberger	8	2
3. Troy Aikman	6	2

As a team player, Roethlisberger had to be happy with being part of a championship. As an individual, he wanted to show he could be a more significant part of that success and not just go down in history as the quarterback with the lowest passing rating while winning a Super Bowl. "It was the months and years after that when you start thinking, man, I played real bad and I didn't help this team win the football game," Roethlisberger said before the game. "That kind of eats at you a little bit. My play didn't help them to win, almost helped them lose it. I expect it to be different this time."[1]

SIGNING UP

In the days following his twenty-sixth birthday, Roethlisberger signed a new eight-year, $102-million

Roethlisberger came into 2008 after playing in his first Pro Bowl.

2008 PITTSBURGH STEELERS GAME-BY-GAME

REGULAR SEASON

9/7, HOUSTON	W, 38–17
9/14, at Cleveland	W, 10–7
9/21, at Philadelphia	L, 6–15
9/29, BALTIMORE	W, 23–20 (OT)
10/5, at Jacksonville	W, 26–21
10/19, at Cincinnati	W, 38–10
10/26, NY GIANTS	L, 14–21
11/3, at Washington	W, 23–6
11/9, INDIANAPOLIS	L, 20–24
11/16, SAN DIEGO	W, 11–10
11/20, CINCINNATI	W, 27–20
11/30, at New England	W, 33–10
12/7, DALLAS	W, 20–13
12/14, at Baltimore	W, 13–9
12/21, at Tennessee	L, 14–31
12/28, CLEVELAND	W, 31–0

PLAYOFFS

1/11, SAN DIEGO	W, 35–24
1/18, BALTIMORE	W, 23–14

SUPER BOWL

2/5, Seattle	W, 21–10

contract with the Pittsburgh Steelers. "This is about being a Pittsburgh Steeler for as long as I can be," Roethlisberger said. "I love Pittsburgh."[2] Roethlisberger said the contract gave him a chance to remain with one team throughout his career as Dan Marino had done with the Miami Dolphins and John Elway had done with the Denver Broncos.

The contract was the largest ever for a Steelers player. "Ben has been an outstanding leader on the field for the Steelers since his rookie year and we are very happy to know that he will be our quarterback for many years to come," Steelers president Art Rooney II said.[3]

ANOTHER CHAMPIONSHIP SEASON

The Pittsburgh Steelers got started on their path toward Super Bowl XLIII with a 38–17 victory over the Houston Texans. The win extended the NFL's longest active opening-day winning streak to six games. Roethlisberger misfired on just one pass, completing 13 of 14 for 167 yards and a pair of touchdowns to Hines Ward.

Pittsburgh's offense combined for just sixteen points in the second and third weeks, but the team managed to split those games. The offense then picked up steam to get the Steelers to 5–1 before falling to the defending Super Bowl champion New York Giants.

As the midway point approached, the season became more difficult for Roethlisberger. The quarterback sat with a sore right shoulder in the second half as his backup, Byron Leftwich, led the team on two long scoring drives that sealed a 23–6 win against the Redskins in Washington, D.C. Roethlisberger played with the injury the following week, but he felt a different kind of pain after his two costly interceptions led to a ten-point lead getting away. The Steelers lost 24–20 to the Indianapolis Colts in Pittsburgh. "If this was an individual sport and I lost the game, I wouldn't feel so bad," Roethlisberger said. "Letting your teammates down, it hurts. I lost this game and it hurts."[5]

> **"If this was an individual sport and I lost the game, I wouldn't feel so bad. Letting your teammates down, it hurts. I lost this game and it hurts."**
>
> —Ben Roethlisberger

The defense led the way for much of the next five weeks, producing four straight wins and keeping the team close enough to pull out a fifth. Roethlisberger continued his habit of fourth-quarter comebacks when he drove the Steelers 92 yards on 12 plays. The drive culminated in Roethlisberger's 4-yard touchdown pass to Santonio Holmes with less than four minutes left for

LATE COMEBACKS

In his first five years in the NFL, Roethlisberger led the Steelers to victory after being behind in the fourth quarter nineteen times. Before rallying the Steelers in Super Bowl XLIII, Roethlisberger brought the team back five times during the 2008 regular season. "We don't like to have to do it," Roethlisberger said. "Normally, you have to do it when you are struggling early on. It comes from the heart. A lot of guys have to step up and not make mistakes and do it when it counts."

a 13–9 win in Baltimore. The Steelers' record improved to 11–3.

Despite the impressive record, there were still some tough times ahead for the Steelers. A loss in Tennessee assured the Titans of the home-field advantage throughout the AFC playoffs. Then, during a 31–0 rout of Cleveland in the final game of the season, Roethlisberger suffered the scariest on-field injury of his career.

Cleveland linebackers D'Qwell Jackson and Willie McGinest hit Roethlisberger as he was releasing a pass late in the first half. Roethlisberger stayed down and was removed from the field on a backboard and stretcher. To try to indicate that he was okay, Roethlisberger gave fans a thumbs-up signal as he left the field. "It happens in football every day," McGinest said, explaining that it was a clean hit. "Ben is a big, aggressive quarterback. He makes a lot of plays and breaks a lot of tackles. When you get him, you gotta get him hard. Nobody intentionally tried to hurt him or anything like that."[6]

The injury was described as either a concussion or a spinal cord concussion, but Roethlisberger was essentially fine. With two weeks before the first play-off game, he was in a position to return.

THE PLAYOFFS

The San Diego Chargers, once a 4–8 team, made a late run to reach the playoffs with four straight victories. They went to Indianapolis and got an overtime win in the wild-card round.

Pittsburgh opened the playoffs by bringing an end to San Diego's five-game winning streak, 35–24. The Chargers scored just 2:01 into the game. Quarterback Philip Rivers passed for more than 100 yards in the first quarter, and San Diego went ahead again briefly in the second quarter. The Steelers, however, moved in front at halftime and dominated the second half, building the lead to eighteen points twice in the second half.

Baltimore defeated Tennessee in the other conference semifinal. The Titans' loss gave the Steelers home-field advantage in the AFC Championship Game. The two close regular-season wins—by three points in overtime and by four points with a fourth-quarter comeback—had given the Steelers the AFC North title over the Ravens. But it had also made it clear that not much separated the teams. "What else would you expect, us and the Ravens?" Pittsburgh coach Mike Tomlin said. "It would be big if it was a scrimmage. This is for the AFC championship."[7] And, along with it, a shot at the Super Bowl.

The Philadelphia Eagles lost to the Arizona Cardinals in the NFC Championship Game, ending the chance for an all-Pennsylvania Super Bowl. Meanwhile, the Steelers took care of the Ravens with the most convincing of the three victories of the season over their rivals, 23–14. Roethlisberger and Santonio Holmes connected on a 65-yard touchdown pass in the second quarter for a 13–0 lead. The Ravens made it interesting late, but Steelers safety Troy Polamalu sealed the win when weaved his way up the field with an interception for a 40-yard touchdown.

THE RETURN TRIP

The Steelers arrived in Tampa, Florida, on January 26 ready to become the first NFL team to win six Super Bowls. Roethlisberger made sure to capture as many memories as possible. He said he had a camera and took about twenty-five pictures the first time he went to the Super Bowl. The second time, he was seen frequently with a camcorder. "I thought to

Roethlisberger records the action during Media Day prior to Super Bowl XLIII.

myself, of all the greats that never had a chance to do this . . . this may be my last one," he said. "I hope not but you never know so I am going to soak it all up, every single minute and just enjoy it because you never know if it is going to happen again."[8]

Roethlisberger spoke openly about how nervous he had been the first time around. He wanted to be sure to relax, both to make the experience as enjoyable as possible, but also to help him perform better under what can be intense pressure. As the game approached, he was in a much better state of mind. "I felt a lot better," Roethlisberger said. "I didn't have the jitters. I actually didn't feel nervous, but then the planes flew over. That's when I was the most nervous."[9]

Linebacker James Harrison's dramatic 100-yard interception return on the final play of the first half gave Pittsburgh a 17–7 lead. But given another chance, Arizona Cardinals veteran quarterback Kurt Warner put the Cardinals into the lead, coming from 13 down in the fourth quarter to go in front, 23–20.

THE DRIVE

When Warner put the Cardinals in front with a long touchdown pass to Larry Fitzgerald Jr., it threatened to ruin the Super Bowl for the Steelers. Instead, Roethlisberger took over. He would play a much different role in his second Super Bowl victory.

Roethlisberger and Super Bowl MVP Holmes led the Steelers on a comeback and game-winning drive. It rivaled the one legendary quarterback Joe Montana led the San Francisco 49ers on twenty years earlier to beat the Cincinnati Bengals in Super Bowl XXIII.

Roethlisberger and the Pittsburgh offense took the field with 2:30 left, needing a field goal to force overtime or a touchdown to win. The now-veteran Steelers quarterback went 5-for-6 for 70 yards on the drive. Three connections with Holmes were the most memorable.

On third-and-six from the Pittsburgh 26, Roethlisberger hit Holmes in tight coverage for 10 yards and a first down to keep the drive alive. When Roethlisberger was tackled on a scramble with 1:02 left, the Steelers needed to call timeout to stop the clock and reorganize. Roethlisberger found Holmes

SUPER SIX

When the Pittsburgh Steelers beat the Arizona Cardinals, 27–23, in Super Bowl XLIII, they became the first team to win six Super Bowls. The San Francisco 49ers and Dallas Cowboys have each won five times. Pittsburgh has won Super Bowls in 1975, 1976, 1979, 1980, 2006, and 2009.

again with a short pass. As Holmes ran toward the sideline with a chance to go out of bounds and stop the clock, he instead kept running—and running. Holmes turned the pass into a 40-yard gain and a first down at the Cardinals' 6.

By not settling for stopping the clock, the Steelers now had a chance to win the game, not just settling for a game-tying field goal. Roethlisberger's only incompletion of the drive stopped the clock with 42 seconds left. On a second try, Roethlisberger lofted the near-perfect pass to the right corner and Holmes made the perfect catch, tapping the toes of both feet in the corner to make it legal. Once the defense held the Cardinals one final time, the Steelers were champions.

"We went from an all-time low to an all-time high, all in three minutes," said Ward, who had been MVP of the Super Bowl XL victory when Roethlisberger struggled.[10] This time, it was the young quarterback who was leading the way for his teammates. "That was probably a drive that will be remembered for a long time in Steeler history," Roethlisberger said.[11]

Roethlisberger celebrates the Steelers' second Super Bowl win in five years.

CAREER ACHIEVEMENTS

- Selected to Pro Bowl following 2007 season

- Youngest starting quarterback to ever win a Super Bowl

- Won two Super Bowls in his first five years in the NFL

- First-round National Football League draft pick (No. 11 overall)

- Had the highest passer rating and completion percentage of any rookie in NFL history

- Won first 15 starts in first year as a professional quarterback

- Holds most passing records at Miami University of Ohio

- Both high school and college football jersey numbers (7) have been retired

- Played in both the Ohio North-South and Big 33 Football Classic high school all-star games

- Captain and league all-star in three sports—football, basketball and baseball—at Findlay High School in Ohio

- Set Ohio state record for passing yards (4,041) and touchdowns (54) in a high school season

- Threw 6 touchdown passes in first game as a starting high school quarterback

CAREER STATISTICS

PASSING

Season	Games	Att.	Comp.	Int.	Yards	TDs	Rating
2004	14	295	196	11	2,621	17	98.1
2005	12	268	168	9	2,385	17	98.6
2006	15	469	280	23	3,513	18	75.4
2007	15	404	264	11	3,154	32	104.1
2008	16	469	281	15	3,301	17	80.1
TOTAL	72	1,905	1,189	69	14,974	101	89.4

RUSHING

Season	Att.	Yards	Avg.	TDs
2004	56	144	2.6	1
2005	31	69	5.8	3
2006	32	98	3.1	2
2007	35	204	5.8	2
2008	34	101	6.3	2
TOTAL	188	616	3.3	10

KEY:
Att. – Attempts
Comp. – Completions
Int. – Interceptions
TDs – Touchdowns
Rating – NFL Passer Rating

FOR MORE INFORMATION

FURTHER READING

Chastain, Bill. *Steel Dynasty: The Team That Changed the NFL*. Chicago, Ill.: Triumph Books, 2005.

Koestler-Grack, Rachel A. *Ben Roethlisberger*. New York: Chelsea House Publishers, 2008.

Wexell, Jim. *Steeler Nation: A Pittsburgh Team, An American Phenomenon*. Irwin, Pa.: Pittsburgh Sports Pub., 2008.

WEB LINKS

Ben Roethlisberger Official Site
www.bigben7.com

Career statistics
www.nfl.com/players/benroethlisberger/
profile?id=ROE750381

CHAPTER NOTES

CHAPTER 1. SUPER BOWL CHAMP

1. Greg Garber, "Steelers get past Seahawks for fifth Super Bowl win in club history," *espn.com*, February 5, 2006. <http://sports.espn.go.com/nfl/recap?gameId=260205023> (October 8, 2008)

2. Garber, February 5, 2006.

3. Larry Weisman, "It's Steel curtains for Seahawks in Super Bowl XL," *USA Today*. February 6, 2006. <http://www.usatoday.com/sports/football/super/2006-02-05-seahawks-steelers_x.htm> (October 8, 2008)

CHAPTER 2. MAKING IT COUNT

1. Mike Wilkening, "Hoeppner, Roethlisberger rose to prominence together," *ProFootballWeekly.com*, June 20, 2007 <http://www.profootballweekly.com/PFW/NFL/AFC/AFC+North/Pittsburgh/Features/2007/wilky062007.htm> (April 27, 2009)

2. Ibid.

3. Ben's Bio. <http://www.bigben7.com/Biography.aspx> (January 1, 2009)

4. David Fleming, "Stainless—Ben Roethlisberger," *ESPN Magazine*, January 31, 2005, <http://insider.espn.go.com/insider/magazine/story?id=1969439> (January 1, 2009)

5. Ibid.

6. Billy Witz, "Ben Wagon—The Town of Findlay, Ohio, Helped Set Roethlisberger's Foundation," 2006, <http://www.thefreelibrary.com/BEN+WAGON+THE+TOWN+OF+FINDLAY,+OHIO,+HELPED+SET+ROETHLISBERGER'S...-a0141653950> (January 1, 2009)

7. Wilkening, June 20, 2007.

CHAPTER 3. COLLEGE CAREER

1. John Erardi, "Flying High, Yet Grounded—Miami's Quarterback An All-American Guy," *Cincinnati Enquirer*, December 18, 2003. <http://bigbennews.com/articles/2003/flyinghigh.html> (January 2, 2009)

2. Ben's Bio. <http://www.bigben7.com/Biography.aspx > (January 1, 2009)

3. John Erardi, "Flying High, Yet Grounded—Miami's Quarterback An All-American Guy," *Cincinnati Enquirer*, December 18, 2003. <http://bigbennews.com/articles/2003/flyinghigh.html> (January 2, 2009)

4. Ben's Bio, January 1, 2009.

5. "Roethlisberger Ends College Career In Style," *Los Angeles Times*, p. D-8, December 19, 2003. <http://articles.latimes.com/2003/dec/19/sports/sp-gmac19 > (February 20, 2009)

CHAPTER NOTES

CHAPTER 4. DRAFT SEASON

1. Tom Dienhart, "Pro rated: meet Ben Roethlisberger, the No. 1 draft prospect at quarterback," *The Sporting News*, September 15, 2003, <http://findarticles.com/p/articles/mi_m1208/is_37_227/ai_107699635> (February 20, 2009)

2. Josh Elliott, "The Sure Thing," *Sports Illustrated-On Campus*, April 15, 2004. <http://www.bigbennews.com/articles/2004/thesurething.html > (January 9, 2009)

3. Mark Curnutte, "QB packs 'em in for a pro workout," *The Cincinnati Enquirer*, March 26, 2004, <http://bengals.enquirer.com/2004/03/26/Ben-0326.html> (February 20, 2009)

4. Elliott, April 15, 2004.

5. Jacob Luft, "Third wheel ," *cnnsi.com*, April 25, 2004, <http://sportsillustrated.cnn.com/2004/football/nfl/specials/draft/2004/04/24/luft.roethlisberger/index.html> (January 16, 2009)

6. Tom Pedulla, "Steelers' Roethlisberger a perfect fit for Super Bowl XL," *USA Today*. February 2, 2008, <http://www.usatoday.com/sports/football/nfl/steelers/2006-02-02-roethlisberger-cover_x.htm> (October 8, 2008)

CHAPTER 5. ROOKIE OF THE YEAR

1. Douglas Lederman, "Roethlisberger stays off his own bandwagon," *USA Today*, October 14, 2004, <http://www.usatoday.com/sports/football/nfl/steelers/2004-10-13-big-ben_x.htm> (January 15, 2009)

2. Dennis Dillon, "Roethlisberger sizzles with meaty performance," *The Sporting News*, November 1, 2004, <http://findarticles.com/p/articles/mi_m1208/is_44_228/ai_n9771317> (January 17, 2009)

3. Paul Attner, "A Cut Above," *The Sporting News*, November 15, 2004, <http://tsn.sportingnews.com/exclusives/20041115/580130.html> (January 18, 2009)

4. Michael A. Fuoco, "Rookie QB Roethlisberger Tops The Menu With Admiring Fans," *Pittsburgh Post-Gazette*, November 4, 2004, <http://www.bigbennews.com/articles/2004/rookieqb.html> (January 18, 2009)

5. Lonnie Wheeler, "Big Man on Campus," *The Cincinnati Post*, November 17, 2004, <http://www.bigbennews.com/articles/2004/bigmanoncampus.html > (January 18, 2009)

6. Attner, November 15, 2004.

7. Ibid.

8. Tom Spousta, "Rookie Roethlisberger Wins Over Everybody," *USA Today*. January 11, 2005. <http://www.usatoday.com/sports/football/nfl/steelers/2005-01-11-big-ben-cover_x.htm > (January 18, 2009)

CHAPTER 6. ROAD TO THE SUPER BOWL

1. Barry Wilner, "Steelers, Ben don't break," *Chicago Sun Times*, January 16, 2006, <http://www.bigbennews.com/articles/2006/steelersbendontbreak.html> (February 6, 2009)

2. Ibid.

3. Ibid.

CHAPTER NOTES

CHAPTER 7. INJURY AND ILLNESS

1. Mark Monroe, "Carlee Roethlisberger has impressive record," *Toledo Blade*, February 15, 2007, <http://toledoblade.com/apps/pbcs.dll/article?AID=/20070215/SPORTS06/702150378/-1/SPORTS09 > (January 1, 2009)

2. Monroe, February 15, 2007.

3. "Big Ben in serious condition after motorcycle accident," June 13, 2006, (February 15, 2009)

4. Ed Bouchette and Gerry Dulac, "Steelers sign St. Pierre as appendectomy sidelines Big Ben," *Pittsburgh Post-Gazette*, September 4, 2006, <http://www.post-gazette.com/pg/06247/718946-66.stm> (February 16, 2009)

5. "At least Roethlisberger knows next season can't be much worse," *The Associated Press*, December 26, 2006, <http://www.pittsburghlive.com/x/pittsburghtrib/sports/steelers/s_485723.html> (February 16, 2009)

6. Ibid.

CHAPTER 8. BUILDING A FOUNDATION

1. Ben Roethlisberger, "Ben Roethlisberger Hands It to Canines," *USA Weekend*, October 21, 2007, <http://www.usaweekend.com/07_issues/071021/071021makeadifferenceday-nfl.html> (February 17, 2009)

2. Jennifer Feehan, "Officer's loss of K-9 partner is soothed with help of new dog," *Toledo Blade*, April 29, 2007, <http://www.toledoblade.com/apps/pbcs.dll/article?AID=/20070429/NEWS17/704290316/0/NEWS24> (February 19, 2009)

3. Roethlisberger, October 21, 2007.

4. "Ben Roethlisberger Foundation," *bigben7.com*, <http://www.bigben7.com/foundation.aspx> (February 17, 2009)

5. Roethlisberger, October 21, 2007.

CHAPTER 9. BACK IN FORM

1. F. Dale Lolley, "With receiving corps depleted, Roethlisberger shows his greatness," *Washington (Pa.) Observer-Reporter*, October 8, 2007, <http://www.observer-reporter.com/OR/Story/10_8_Steelers_Hawks_column> (February 18, 2009)

2. John Harris, "Steelers' Big Ben has mistake-free day," *Pittsburgh Tribune-Review*, September 10, 2007, <http://www.pittsburghlive.com/x/pittsburghtrib/sports/steelers/s_526593.html> (February 18, 2009)

3. Ibid.

4. Danny O'Neil, "Steelers QB just rolling with punches of his position," *Seattle Times*. October 7, 2007, <http://seattletimes.nwsource.com/html/seahawks/2003930428_hawk07.html> (February 18, 2009)

5. Chuck Ludwig, "New coaches turn Roethlisberger loose," *Dayton Daily News*, October 26, 2007, <http://www.daytondailynews.com/s/content/oh/story/sports/pro/bengals/2007/10/25/ddn102607bengals.html?cxtype=rss&cxsvc=7&cxcat=25> (February 18, 2009)

6. Lee Jenkins, "This One's For Hep," *Sports Illustrated*, October 30, 2007, <http://sportsillustrated.cnn.com/2007/writers/lee_jenkins/10/30/big.ben1105/> (February 18, 2009)

7. Ibid.

CHAPTER NOTES

8. Mike Prisuta, "Steelers' Arians proud of Roethlisberger's rally," *Pittsburgh Tribune-Review*, January 9, 2008, <http://livesite. pittsburghlive.com/x/tribunereview/s_546489.html> (February 18, 2009)

CHAPTER 10. SECOND CHANCE

1. Ohm Youngmisuk, "Ben Roethlisberger planning to strike his Super Bowl flop from memory," *New York Daily News*, January 26, 2009, <http://www.nydailynews.com/sports/football/2009/01/ 26/2009-01-26_ben_roethlisberger_planning_to_strike_hi.html> (February 19, 2009)

2. Smith, March 3, 2008.

3. Ibid.

4. Ibid.

5. Scott Brown, "Interceptions ignite Colts' comeback," *Pittsburgh Tribune-Review*, November 10, 2008, <http://www.pittsburghlive .com/x/pittsburghtrib/sports/steelers/s_597676.html> (February 19, 2009>

6. Brown, December 29, 2008.

7. "Offense comes alive as Steelers roll into AFC Championship Game," *The Associated Press*. <http://sports.espn.go.com/nfl/recap?gameId=290111023> (February 19, 2009)

8. Youngmisuk, January 26, 2009.

9. Tim Smith, "Ben Roethlisberger is Super this time leading game-winning drive for Steelers," *New York Daily News*, February 1, 2009, <http://www.nydailynews.com/sports/football/2009/02/01/2009-02-01_ben_roethlisberger_is_super_this_time_le.html> (February 19, 2009)

GLOSSARY

blitz—A tactic in which the defense uses linebackers or defensive backs to rush the passer.

bowl game—Postseason college football games in which top teams are invited to participate.

concussion—A brain injury, usually caused by a blow to the head, in which the brain shakes inside the skull.

draft—A process in which professional sports teams choose players in order.

red zone—The area inside an opponent's 20-yard line.

redshirt—The process in which a college athlete sits out a year of competition while studying and practicing. The redshirt year does not count against the four years the player is allowed to compete.

rookie—A first-year professional.

sack—When a quarterback is tackled before he can pass.

scholarship—A grant of money to a student for educational purposes; top athletes are offered scholarships by colleges to attend and play sports for their schools.

scramble—When a football team plans to pass, but the quarterback winds up running to avoid pass rushers.

shotgun—A football formation in which the ball is snapped through the air to the quarterback, who is several yards behind the center.

INDEX

INDEX

JB ROETHLISBERGER
Robinson, Tom.
Ben Roethlisberger

3-5-10